Crash Course in Corporate Communications

ALSO BY RACHEL MCALPINE

Books about writing
Nine WinningHabits of Successful Authors
Web Word Wizardry
The Passionate Pen
Global English for Global Business
Real Writing
Song in the Satchel

Fiction
Farewell Speech
Running Away from Home
The Limits of Green

Poetry
Another 100 New Zealand Poems for Children (Editor)
Tourist in Kyoto
Selected Poems
Thirteen Waves
Recording Angel
House Poems
Fancy Dress
Stay at the Dinner Party
Lament for Ariadne

Plays
The Dazzling Night: A Noh play in English
Power Play
Peace Offering
Driftwood
The Stationary Sixth Form Poetry Trip

Textbooks for ESL students
The Great New Zealand Study Trip
Katherine Mansfield in New Zealand
Masako in New Zealand
The Secret Life of New Zealand

Children's fiction
Maria in the Middle

Crash Course in Corporate Communications

Rachel McAlpine

CORPORATE COMMUNICATIONS

Published by Corporate Communications
PO Box 6559, Wellington, New Zealand
www.webpageecontent.com
office@writing.co.nz

ISBN 0-473-06017-5

First published 1999, reprinted 2002
9 8 7 6 5 4 3 2 1

Rachel McAlpine is a writer, editor and trainer specialising in Web writing. She lives in Wellington, New Zealand.

Sponsor's foreword

Advanced Business
Education Limited

'A clever person finds a solution to a problem. A wise person avoids it'. Albert Einstein.

The key to avoiding or solving many business problems is good communication. It is the oil that makes the corporate machine function.

There is almost endless research that demonstrates communication, both verbal and written, is a critical factor in successful business. As business styles have become more open, more democratic, more egalitarian, and more 'team based', the need for quality in the communication process has become even more of an imperative for the successful business.

This emphasis on quality communication has been recognised by the Institute of Chartered Accountants of New Zealand in its Professional Competence Programme. All persons seeking to become members of the Institute must complete the relevant sections of this Programme, which is offered by Advanced Business Education Limited (a wholly owned subsidiary of the Institute). Competence in both written and verbal communication is a key focus of the assessment undertaken in this Programme.

In order to provide a communications resource for candidates of the Programme, Advanced Business Education Limited approached Rachel McAlpine to develop a practical, easy-to-use guide to good business communication. The result—*Crash Course in Corporate Communications.*

As those who have already been issued with the guide now use it as a day to day resource in the workplace, it will further realise its potential to make a real difference to standards of business communication.

The style and 'user-friendliness' of the guide is a reflection of Rachel's own professionalism and ability as a communicator. Needless to say Advanced Business Education Limited is delighted with the result and endorses the guide to its candidates. It also thoroughly recommends *Crash Course in Corporate Communications* to others as a handy reference tool to improve their written and verbal communication skills.

Good writing, speaking and listening!

W Gill Cox

Executive Director

Advanced Business Education Limited

Table of contents

1

First things first

Corporate communications

Corporate communications staff are wordsmiths, PR practitioners, journalists and marketers. Their job description expands every year. The corporate communications department or company is constantly evolving in response to new technology and changes in business practice.

Not so long ago, wordsmiths could remain aloof from technology. Artists could sneer at computers. Technicians could ignore aesthetics and language. PR officers didn't bother about mundane things like in-house memos. Human resources staff could ignore their influence on profits. Quality control of documentation was often non-existent. And archiving was done by the lowliest employee shuffling around a basement of dusty paper files.

That's all changed now, and technology has driven the changes. In these hectic times we're all obliged to keep extending the boundaries of our knowledge—or be left behind. Virtually everyone in an organisation is involved in communication, and the cost of poor communication is steep.

How to use this manual

'Excellent communication skills' is now a requirement for most jobs from middle management upwards. Use *Crash Course in Corporate Communications* to upgrade your own skills or train your staff.

This is a complete manual for corporate communications. It starts with the plain English basics. Then it shows you how to write anything from humble e-mails to major proposals and policy documents—dealing with content, style and design. Chapter 8 is about oral communication in the corporate environment. Chapter 9 tells you all you need to know about editing and grammar. Chapter 10 introduces the broader responsibilities of corporate communications staff, such as developing a documentation policy.

So much to write—so little time! You're always in a hurry. You're in a hurry right now—maybe you're about to start writing a memo or a major proposal or a technical manual. And unless you're a full-time student, you have little time to spend on improving your writing.

That's why this is a crash course. Just read the book through once. (Naturally, it's easy to read.) Then scan the relevant part of the book:

- whenever you get stuck or confused in your writing
- whenever you need to write a new type of document
- when you're about to start writing an important document
- when you must tackle a new corporate communications taskß.

Templates, checklists and good examples at the back are designed for quick and easy reference.

In *Crash Course in Corporate Communications* the emphasis is on useful rules of thumb—not on theory. Tips that will save you annoyance and embarrassment. Tips on avoiding grammar mistakes. Tips to speed up the writing process.

Of course, you will also find some explanations of the principles of good writing, because it's easier to remember rules if you understand the reasons.

Is this you?

'I can't write. I hate writing.' Relax! This manual makes it easy. All the help you need is in these pages. When you understand the principles of plain English, you'll find that writing has never been easier.

'It takes me so long to write anything.' *Crash Course in Corporate Communication* includes many tips on writing faster.

'I don't know anything about grammar.' That's OK. You don't need to swallow a grammar book in order to write correctly. All you need to know is how to avoid the commonest mistakes.

'I've been writing business documents for forty years.' A new business environment and new technology have influenced the format and style of business documents. What was correct yesterday may seem old-fashioned or confusing today. This manual will bring you right up to date.

'I'm a technical writer. Is this book specialised enough to help me?'
Technical writers will find significant help throughout this book. Almost every chapter contains relevant advice.

Technical writing includes any documents with a technical or scientific dimension, such as:

- procedures and instructions
- ISO9001 documentation
- any writing about a technical or scientific subject
- training materials
- feasibility studies and progress reports
- action plans.

However, if you're writing or editing the content for Web pages, you need *Web Word Wizardry*.[1] The Web copywriter needs to ensure that Web pages are findable, scannable, understandable, credible and profitable. Writing Web or Intranet copy is quite complex, but *Web Word Wizardry* makes it easy.

The cost of poor communication

The reputation of your organisation is enhanced by clear writing and good presentation. Documents that are incomprehensible, late, or incorrect can do your company an astonishing amount of damage. In fact, poor communication can have a major impact on your profits.

Difficult texts and slack communications systems cause:

- misunderstandings
- errors
- complaints
- unnecessary inquiries
- staff time lost to problem solving.

Even simple letters can cost your organisation thousands of dollars every year. If your customers receive an ambiguous or incomplete or badly worded letter, they may throw the letter away. Or they may phone with inquiries or protests, or act on what they wrongly assume to be the meaning.

---

[1] *Web Word Wizardry* by Rachel McAlpine. ISBN 1-58008-223-8

Research on the hidden costs of poor communication

Cost and time benefits studies in the US and Britain have shown that about 40% of most organisations' resources are consumed by communication. Writing in plain English (also called plain language) saves money.

According to Jack Gillespie and Isabelle Bruder Smith:

> Inadequate communication wastes 14% of every 40 hour week. That's according to a survey of executives at 1,000 of the largest US firms by Office Team, the Menlo Park, California staffing service. And that amounts to a whopping seven weeks each year.[2]

A 1996 nationwide survey by the Australian Bureau of Statistics revealed that 14 per cent of people—including those who speak English as a first language—need help with reading information from government agencies, businesses and other institutions.

Insurance companies in the Canada, US, UK and Australia report that customer relations have improved dramatically, and profitability has increased as a result of using plain English.

Canada[3]

1. One of the largest insurance companies redesigned a standard claim form. The project resulted in a 90% reduction in the number of customised claim forms.

2. After the Royal Insurance Company of Canada unveiled its 'simple English' home insurance policy, sales increased by 38% in one year, from $58 million to $79 million.

3. The Ontario Ministry of Education and Training used plain English when redesigning the application form for the Ontario Student Assistance Program. The new form takes 50% less time to process.

4. The provincial government in British Columbia used plain English in all new Small Claims Court acts and rules of court, and all new court forms and brochures. The court registrar now handles 40% more cases with the same number of staff.

---

[2] *In The Loop*, May 1999, International Association of Business Communicators in NZ.

[3] Information from The Plain Language Center, Toronto. Information Management and Economics Inc., 1996.

Australia

1. The Australian police summons form was redesigned and rewritten in a simpler style. As a result, staff were freed for other work, and staff numbers were reduced. Savings in salaries: about AUD$400,000 a year.

2. The Capita Insurance Company studied errors made on 17 different application forms. The annual cost of those errors was AUD$551,465. For less than AUD$100,000, the forms were amalgamated and simplified. The error rate dropped by 97.2 per cent, which saved over AUD$500,000 of staff time in one year.

3. After the Family Court of Australia simplified its divorce application form, forms rejected because of errors dropped from 30 per cent to 7 per cent.

Britain

1. The Department of Defence redesigned an internal expense claim form. The new form cost about US$15,000 to produce and saved about US$475,000 a year.

2. A plain English application form for legal aid was introduced in the UK. It cost about US$50,000 to develop and test, and saves almost US$3,000,000 in staff time each year.

USA

The Federal Communications Commission once had five full-time staff answering questions about regulations governing citizen's band radios. After the regulations were rewritten in plain English, the questions stopped and the staff were reassigned.

The history of plain English

Maybe the drive for plain English started in 1525 when William Tyndale began printing his English translation of the New Testament. This was a radical step. Before that, only the élite in Britain could read and write—and they used Latin.

The American, Canadian, and British governments have plain English policies. In 1990, International Literacy Year, the Australian government launched several initiatives to promote the use of plain English in all sectors.

In the 1960s, US consumer groups stimulated legislation on plain English. Richard Nixon decreed in 1972 that the Federal Register be written in 'layman's terms', and President Carter issued an Executive Order 'to make

Federal regulations clearer, less burdensome, and more cost effective.' Seven states have passed laws to regulate the comprehensibility of consumer contracts; laws have been passed in twenty-eight states to control the readability and usability of insurance contracts.

The battle continues against gobbledegook in business, legal and government documents. On 1 June 1998 President Clinton wrote:

> **SUBJECT: Plain Language in Government Writing**
>
> The Vice President and I have made reinventing the Federal Government a top priority of my Administration. We are determined to make the Government more responsive, accessible and understandable in its communications with the public.
>
> The Federal Government's writing must be in plain language. By using plain language, we send a clear message about what the Government is doing, what it requires, and what services it offers. Plain language saves the Government and the private sector time, effort and money.
>
> Plain language requirements vary from one document to another, depending on the intended audience. Plain language documents have logical organization, easy-to-read design features, and use:
>
> - common, everyday words, except for necessary technical terms;
> - 'you' and other pronouns;
> - the active voice; and
> - short sentences.
>
> To ensure the use of plain language, I direct you to do the following...

How plain English helps

How does plain English help you, the writer? Plain English:

- creates a positive, professional image
- provides better quality information for management
- saves staff time spent on inquiries, complaints, and processing forms
- saves printing costs
- makes it easier to translate documents into other languages.

How does plain English help your customer or reader? Plain English:

- prevents misunderstandings
- saves time and frustration caused by having to ask for help
- makes it easier to fill in forms
- gives people positive feelings about your company or organisation.

2

Write plain English

'Use short sentences, use short paragraphs, use vigorous English, not forgetting to strive for smoothness. Be positive, not negative.' Ernest Hemingway

Plain in two ways

Anything written in plain English is plain in two ways.

1. The meaning is plain. It's crystal clear and obvious—not unclear, obscure, ambiguous, hidden or confused.

2. The language is plain. Familiar, ordinary, common words are used. The words are not fancy, complicated, or elaborate. The style is not literary or intricate. The same word is used consistently for the same thing.

Plain English is much more than just a simplified style of writing. Plain English also rationalises document design and the organisation of ideas.

Throughout this book, 'fancy' is a dirty word!

Documents that should be in plain English

1. all legislation
2. all regulations
3. documents explaining government policies and laws
4. legal documents including leases, contracts and financial agreements
5. forms of all kinds, including applications for government payments, loan and credit card applications, taxation forms and hospital admission forms

6. government reports
7. insurance policies, applications and renewal forms
8. brochures, leaflets and booklets
9. letters from banks, government departments and other organisations
10. bills, such as phone and gas bills
11. computer manuals
12. instructions for using products such as electrical appliances
13. information about drugs and medicines
14. corporate rule books and policy manuals
15. tenders and specifications
16. training materials, memos, procedures and quality assurance manuals
17. annual reports and other reports
18. newsletters
19. all notices and signs
20. airline and public transport timetables.

Main features of plain English

1. Plain English documents are written for the reader, not the writer.
2. Familiar, simple vocabulary is used.
3. Simple grammatical structures are preferred.
4. Plain English documents are concise.
5. The content is in a logical sequence.
6. Documents are easily read and understood by their intended readers.
7. Documents have easy-to-read design features.
8. Grammar, spelling and punctuation are accurate and consistent throughout the text.

Write for the reader

Plain English documents are always written, structured and designed expressly for the reader. The reader comes first! This is the number one feature of plain English. In fact, it is the reason for all the other features.

Always keep the reader's needs in mind as you plan and write a document. See everything from the reader's point of view. For example, if your document is intended for technical readers, you can use technical or specialised terms (and still write plain English). But if your document is intended for the general public, you will use terms familiar to the lay person, or at least explain technical terms.

Even complex concepts can be explained in plain English. Many legal documents, such as contracts and legislation, have been rewritten in plain English and are still legally accurate.

You may need to rethink the structure and purpose of your document. Ask yourself:

- Is this document really necessary?
- Who am I 'talking' to in this document?
- What do readers need to know?
- What do they need to know first?
- How much do they understand about the subject?
- What's the best way to organise these ideas for the reader?

With a plain language document, the intended readers can understand the message. More important, they can understand it on their first attempt.

Use familiar, simple vocabulary

In your business writing, use:

- common, simple words except for necessary technical terms
- words with a clear meaning
- single words instead of wordy phrases
- the same word for the same thing—don't search for a more 'interesting' alternative, but be consistent.

'You' and 'please' and 'thank you' are three powerful ways to communicate clearly. When you start a sentence with either 'You' or 'Please' or 'Thank you', that sentence will most probably be easy to write and easy to understand. Better still, you'll write it quickly. It's hard to get into a tangle using these wonderful words.

'You', 'me', 'we' and 'us' make it plain who is saying what. The writer is 'I'. The reader is 'you'. The writer's company or organisation is 'we'.

Cut out fancy phrases!

FANCY PHRASES	PLAIN ENGLISH
with regard to	about
in lieu of	instead of
by means of	by
in the event that	if
in the region of	about
until such time as	until
during such time as	while
in view of the fact	because
on the part of	by
subsequent to	after
under the provisions of	under
with a view to	to
it would appear that	apparently
it is probable that	probably
notwithstanding the fact that	although
adequate number of	enough
excessive number of	too many

Use simple grammatical structures

Don't try to write fancy sentences!

Plain English makes life easy for you by insisting on simple grammatical structures. When you acquire this habit, you'll write more quickly. You can stop stressing out over complicated grammatical rules. Instead, use:

- short sentences
- more action verbs and fewer abstract nouns
- active verbs
- logically structured sentences
- positive language.[4]

Most of your sentences turn out OK, don't they? If they seem right, they probably are right. Your instincts are usually fairly trustworthy, if you learned English as your first language.

By the same token, if you think there's something wrong with a sentence, there probably is. Take another look at the one that bothers you. Can you say it more simply? Of course you can. And is that sentence really necessary? If in doubt, cut it out.

[4] All these terms are explained in this chapter.

Use short sentences

Short sentences communicate powerfully. Writing short sentences is a very good trick.

Plain English uses short sentences. If you write short sentences, your meaning is usually clear and your grammar is usually correct. It's that simple.

Aim for an average of 16-20 words per sentence in business documents. For direct marketing and advertising, no sentence should be longer than 16 words. For procedures, cut sentences short at 20 words. For broad policy documents and academic writing, your average sentence length can be a little longer than 20 words.

EASY FIX

The danger point occurs at 20 words. If you are having trouble writing a particular sentence, it's probably too long. Just chop it into two or more sentences. Or shorten the sentence by removing unnecessary words.

When counting the number of words in a sentence, regard a capitalised title as a single word. For example, this counts as a three-word sentence:

> The Representative of Public Sector Grammarians resigned.

When you write complete documents, vary the length of your sentences. Too many short sentences in a row can become boring for the reader.

And it's fine to start a sentence with 'And'. But it's equally legitimate to start a sentence with 'But'. You read such sentences every day in the newspaper, in advertising, in letters and in books. Sentences starting with 'And...' or 'But...' are common in Shakespeare and the Bible.

Use more action verbs and fewer abstract nouns

A verb is a 'doing' word. Examples of action verbs:

> jump, edit, write, hurry, explode, sign, resign

Where there's an action verb, there's action! And where there's action, the writing is easy to understand. It races along. (The verb 'be' and 'have' are also verbs, but they're not action verbs. They're fine, but different.)

Nouns are names of things. If there's an overload of nouns, the action stops. Nothing happens. You're writing a list, not a readable sentence.

Abstract nouns are names of things you cannot see—like 'peace', 'rationalisation', 'discernment', 'sensitivity'. If there's an overload of abstract nouns in your writing, the meaning becomes woolly and vague, because it's hard to imagine a lot of abstract ideas at once.

Most abstract nouns began life as a busy, active, easy-to-understand verb.

PLAIN VERB	FANCY ABSTRACT NOUN
construct	construction
rationalise	rationalisation
sense	sensitivity

Corporatespeak is the butt of many jokes, and rightly so. With the worst corporatespeak you find yourself smothering in abstract nouns:

> demutualisation, allocation, privatisation, outcomes, evaluation, resources, deliverables, deinstitutionalise, cup-of-tea-isation...

Naturally some of these words are necessary, but in a corporate environment it is only too easy to slip into very bad habits.

How can you tell when you have started talking gobbledegook? It's a sure sign when an outsider, after reading a few paragraphs, still hasn't got the faintest inkling about what sort of business is being discussed. For example, is the following sentence discussing a chain of hot-dog stands, an accountancy company, a public hospital or the national archives? It could be anything.

> Management will consider the reallocation of resources, the prioritisation of service delivery, and the optimisation of deliverables for the client.

Whenever possible, use a concrete noun like 'frankfurter', 'disease', 'tax' or 'book'. Concrete nouns are the opposite of abstract nouns: they refer to something real that you can see or hear. Concrete nouns help you to keep your feet on the ground. Ordinary people know what a book or a hot-dog is. But concepts like 'reallocation of resources' are highly abstract, and could mean almost anything from closing down a hot-dog stand in Queen Street to transferring a receptionist to another city.

That's OK when you're talking to each other, for example when two managers are discussing policy. But when communicating with the general public, such terms need translating.

EASY FIX

Look for words ending in:

> -tion, -ment, -tion, -ance, -ence, -ance, ancy, -ency, -ity, -ism.

Most such words are abstract nouns. If you have two or more in a sentence, try changing some back into verbs. This is the Plain English way. Notice how the sentence gets shorter.

FANCY	The company now has the capability to achieve evaluation of the results.
PLAIN	The company can now evaluate the results.

ANOTHER EASY FIX

Use concrete nouns wherever possible. Just rewrite the odd sentence so that you can include a word like 'secretary', 'stationery' or 'hotdog'—something people can see in their minds.

Use simple verbs

Try to use short, simple verbs. Don't use fancy, long-winded verbs like 'might have been'. Instead of 'They might have been delayed' you could say, 'They were probably delayed'.

Beware of 'should', 'might', 'shall' and 'will'.

FANCY	If I might suggest a solution.
PLAIN	I suggest...
FANCY	Should you do this...
PLAIN	If you do this...

Use active verbs

As your grammar checker constantly implies, passive verbs are generally regarded as undesirable in business writing. Wherever possible, use active verbs instead. Passive verbs are a little bit fancy.[5]

All verbs are either active or passive.

When the verb is active, the subject of the sentence :

- either actively does something
- or is something.

Active verbs	The CEO (subject) will sign (verb) the agreement.
	The CEO (subject) provides (verb) professional credibility.
	The CEO (subject) was travelling (verb) to Paris yesterday.
	The CEO (subject) is (verb) exceptionally gifted.

When the verb is passive, the subject of the sentence is passive: the subject has something done to it. The subject does not act but is acted upon.

[5] And remember, in this book 'fancy' is a dirty word.

Passive verbs	The agreement (subject) will be signed (verb) by the CEO. OR The CEO (subject) was fired (verb) last Tuesday.

Why are active verbs usually better?

Active verbs make active, vigorous writing.
Active verbs put people in the picture.
Active verbs are shorter and clearer.

Active verbs are natural in the classic English sentence structure:

SOMEBODY (or something) DOES SOMETHING (or is something).

What's wrong with passive verbs? Nothing. But if you have too many passive verbs in a document:

- the meaning can be unclear
- important information can be omitted—namely who does what
- the tone can be unfriendly, cold and official
- the writer can seem evasive or untrustworthy
- sentences are often longer
- sentences can easily get out of control.

Heavily passive writing is like people who are passive all the time. If people never take the initiative or expresses a clear opinion, they can seem irritating, hard work, depressing and even devious. You wonder what they are really thinking...

It's usually OK to have:

- up to 5% passive verbs in advertising or direct marketing documents
- up to 20% passive verbs in business writing
- 20-40% passive verbs in policy documents for discussion.

When should you use passive verbs?

You need passive verbs whenever:

- it is irrelevant who does or did something
- you don't know who does or did something
- for legal or other reasons you don't want to say who does or did something
- it would be tactless to say who does or did something
- the style is smoother in the passive.

GRAMMAR (you can skip this)

How can you recognise a passive verb? A passive verb always has at least two words. The last word is the main verb ending in a past form like 'ed'. The second-last word of the helping verb is always one of these: 'am', 'is', 'are', 'was', 'were', 'be', 'being' or 'been'.

(If the last word ends in '-ing' it's not a passive verb. If the second-last word is 'have', 'has', 'had' or 'having', it's not a passive verb.)

PASSIVE VERBS

is removed
are justified
was spilled
were reminded
will be summoned
is astonished
were sent
will have been spoilt
might have been taken

Structure sentences logically

Don't try to be literary as you construct your sentences. Write plain, ordinary sentences, not fancy ones. The goal in corporate communications is to write clearly.

As Winston Churchill said, 'the essential structure of the ordinary British sentence... is a noble thing.' In the ordinary British sentence, the words go in this order:

1. SOMEBODY or SOMETHING (subject)
2. DOES or IS (subject)
3. SOMETHING (object or complement)
4. extra information if any.

Use this as your default sentence structure. Start sentences with their real subject, not some irrelevant or fancy phrase. You're not trying for the Nobel Prize in Literature. You are trying to write quickly, clearly and correctly. Whenever you are struggling with a sentence, go back to your basic English sentence structure: 'Somebody does something.'

How many ideas should there be in a sentence? One idea in a sentence is enough. Two is plenty. Three ideas usually create confusion. (By the way, a clause is an idea, a sentence, or a sentence-within-a-sentence.)

In a two-idea sentence, put the ideas in their logical order. This is a crude but useful rule of thumb: put 'if' and 'when' clauses first, and 'because' and 'so that' clauses second.

PLAIN	If the coup succeeds, we will need new uniforms.
FANCY	We will need new uniforms if the coup succeeds.
PLAIN	She is visiting Paul because he is sick.
FANCY	Because he is sick, she is visiting Paul.
PLAIN	They have ordered a modem so that they can go on the Internet.
FANCY	So that they can go on the Internet, they have ordered a modem.

EASY FIX

Never use more than one of these words per sentence:

although, because, if, since, unless, but, yet.

FANCY	Although the roadworks are essential, the noise is disturbing the residents but they are tolerating it without complaint.
PLAIN	The noise is disturbing the residents. They are tolerating the noise without complaint because they know the roadworks are essential.

(So 'noise' is repeated? In corporate communications, that's good! People read faster when you use the same word for the same thing.)

Don't overuse phrases like 'It is...' 'There are...' 'It was...' 'It has...' 'There is...' 'There was...' 'There were...' 'There has...' 'There have...'

'It' and 'There' are called false subjects. Sentences that begin with a false subject:

- are often hard to finish writing
- are longer than necessary
- can lose focus.

Naturally it's OK to break this rule occasionally. (I just did.) But don't make a habit of it.

Problems with 'which'

For some reason, sentences containing 'which' frequently cause confusion. Ambiguity is common in 'which' sentences. Be alert to the dangers, and eliminate 'which' when necessary.

UNCLEAR	A security warning has been placed on this account, which will be cancelled once delivery has been confirmed.

Will the security warning be cancelled? Or will the account be cancelled? There's no logical, fail-safe way the reader can know for certain. Knowing the correct grammar rules is no advantage, because the rules themselves are confusing and contradictory. Instead, say what you mean in two stages.

PLAIN	A security warning has been placed on this account. We will cancel this account when delivery has been confirmed.
PLAIN	A security warning has been placed on this account. We will cancel the security warning when delivery has been confirmed.

Problems of clarity also arise with 'that' (though not so frequently).

FANCY	Testing is required to confirm that those fields that permit user data entry do so, and conversely that those that do not also meet that criteria.
PLAIN	The fields permitting data entry must actually permit data entry. The fields not permitting data entry must not permit data entry. We must test to confirm both points.

When you're writing normal business documents, you will certainly need to use 'which' and 'that' sometimes—so be aware of the problems. Keep 'which' and 'that' sentences short. Never use 'that' or 'which' more than once in a sentence. Whenever you write 'which', test the sentence for ambiguity. Show it to several colleagues: do they all understand your meaning? If not, rewrite the sentence. (To check the grammar of 'which' and 'that', see Chapter 9.)

Use positive language

If you want to communicate clearly, use positive language. If you want to confuse people, state something in a negative way. Negative language is dangerous because it has:

- conceptual difficulties (you're writing about something nonexistent)
- psychological difficulties (negative language makes people feel bad)
- cultural implications (negativity can damage international business relationships).

Be especially careful to avoid using:

- two or more negatives in one sentence
- negative language in forms (application forms etc.)
- 'not only... but also'
- negative questions.

Negative words:

no, not, won't, never, nowhere, never, nothing, nobody, no-one etc.

Negative bits of words:

un-, de-, dis-, non-, in-, contra-, counter-. anti- and -less.

Words with negative connotations or complications:

however, except, unless, only if, despite, default, remove, cancel, unfortunately, hesitate, refuse, withdraw, error, loss, poor etc.

FANCY	Please do not hesitate to call me.
PLAIN	Please call me.
UNCLEAR	Do you agree that the number of police should not fall below the number employed nationally as at 31 January 1997?
PLAIN	Do you agree that the number of police officers employed nationally should be at least 8000? (*It's better to be specific as well as positive.*)

Write concisely

Plain English documents are concise. They convey the necessary information and no more. (We're saving trees here.)

Strategies that help you to write concisely include:

- using 'you', 'please' and 'thank you'
- getting rid of fluffy phrases
- replacing abstract nouns with verbs
- using mostly active verbs
- writing short sentences
- writing logically structured sentences
- using positive language.

Organise material logically

Logical structure is a powerful tool in plain English. When items are in the most logical order, people can read and grasp your message quickly. This is such an important aspect of plain English that virtually every chapter of *Crash Course on Corporate Communications* gives guidelines on structure.

Meantime, follow these general rules:

- organise ideas in a logical sequence
- put the main idea or summary first
- have only one idea per paragraph
- put the main idea in a paragraph first
- use plenty of explanatory headings.

Start with the most important item! When you structure your document, remember that the people who read your document are nearly always in a hurry, and they would rather avoid reading your deathless prose. They'd rather be eating oysters (or even mashed potatoes).

Plain English begins and ends with the needs of the reader. The following are all logical systems of organising information, depending entirely on the reader's needs. A large document will use a combination of these systems:

- from most important to least important (this is your default system)
- in chronological order, or step by step
- in analytical order (e.g. comparing two problems or solutions)
- in geographical order (e.g. north to south, top floor to bottom floor)
- from specific to general, or vice versa
- from good news to bad news to good news.

Structure can make or break communication. Many people decide whether to read or dump a business letter after scanning only two things: the first sentence and the signature. If the first sentence is irrelevant, the remainder never gets read. Similarly, with a report, many people read only the executive summary. So it's critical to start every document the right way.

Plain English is easily understood by its intended reader

Plain English documents must be easy to read. If they are intended for the general public, that means people with about 11 years' schooling.

Even highly educated people usually prefer easy-to-read documents. Many CEOs and politicians are obliged to read a huge stack of documents every week. Stressed and busy professionals often put difficult documents aside for later or simply never read them.

A document will usually be easy to read if it has:

- short sentences (an average of 16-20 words per sentence)
- not too many long words (words with three syllables or more).

Count the number of words that appear on one line of your document. Learn how to judge automatically if a sentence has more than 20 words. (The occasional longer sentence is OK provided it is well constructed.)

Fortunately your grammar checker can assess the readability of your document. For example, Microsoft Word gives you a choice of four methods.

The Flesch Reading Ease Index gives a score from 1-100. Think of a 'score' as a percentage, and for normal business writing, aim for 60-70. This means that 60-70% of readers can readily understand your document.

The Flesch-Kincaid Grade Level, the Coleman-Liau Grade Level and the Bormuth Grade Level all state the level of school education required to

understand your document. So if your document has a grade of 10.0, it can be understood by a person with 10 years schooling. (Picture someone whose education finished at the age of 15 or 16.)

GRADE LEVEL	SUITABLE FOR
18 +	for practical purposes this is unreadable
15-17	post-graduate assignments
13-14	reports, articles and books for experts in the same field
11-12	business and government documents, newspapers, magazines
9-10	popular novels, direct marketing, forms
8 or below	children's books

In the end, there is only one valid test of success: do the intended readers understand the document on their first attempt?

When in doubt, simplify your document. The educational level is not the only factor to consider. Remember that people are very likely reading your document:

- in a hurry
- under stress
- with little interest in what you write
- with other things on their mind.

At your workplace you may need to rewrite standard forms and letters, and documents that must communicate clearly to a large number of people. In these cases, it's important to systematically test the documents on real people, the kind of people who will read or use these documents.

3

Everyday communication

'I would have written you a short letter, but I didn't have time.' Winston Churchill—or George Bernard Shaw—or Claude Pascal—or Alexander Pope—or somebody else.[6]

Make the most of e-mail

E-mail is an amazing means of communication. However did we manage without it? E-mail combines most of the advantages of letters and phone calls, with few of their problems.

The e-mail culture does have some problems and drawbacks, though. To make the most of e-mail, you need to communicate clearly, avoid irritating the other person, and be ultra-careful to avoid errors of judgement or fact.

People at work tend to read e-mail in a steaming hurry. If an e-mail isn't relevant or useful, they want to dump it or forward it, preferably without even opening it. Therefore, you must write the perfect subject line.

The perfect subject line:

- is more like a newspaper headline than a traditional heading
- is very specific
- is not too long (so it fits in the space available)
- changes with every e-mail (none of this Re: re: re:...)
- mentions your recipient's name if an office address is shared.

[6] This comment is attributed to a remarkably large number of famous and witty individuals.

PLAIN Data projector required
Charles Smith: trip to Brunei
Wanted — Brazil contacts
Impact seminar series #5 Sydney 22 June
Professor Teele arrives Tuesday
Agenda, Social Committee meeting 22 Nov

UNCLEAR yours of 12 Feb
Re: your services
Re: re: re: re: stuff
Bill
contacts

E-mail seems informal—but don't be careless

Communication by e-mail is so quick and easy that it is often surprisingly casual.

Your professional reputation is at stake when you do business by e-mail. Always double-check what you have written, and never send an e-mail in anger or haste. Ancient e-mails that you have 'deleted' can be retrieved from your computer and used as evidence in court. What you write in an e-mail has as much legal significance as the contents of a letter.

You may be communicating with people in another country or culture. If they begin e-mails with 'Dear Mr Jacobitz,' and finish with 'Yours sincerely,' it's a good idea to reply in kind. If your correspondent takes a formal approach, you may offend by being too casual.

Start simply. You can treat an e-mail like a fax and have no hello-phrase at all. 'Hi Judy' is casual and very common. Any salutation you'd use in a letter is perfectly acceptable.

As with a letter, acknowledge the trail to this e-mail in one sentence.

> Thanks for your order of 12 August 99.
> Yesterday we discussed a problem with your TT500 photocopier.

Limit yourself to one topic per e-mail, if possible.

Keep the format plain. Beware of sending anything fancy if you don't know your reader's business environment. Some systems won't deliver any e-mails with attachments. Other sytems show a blank message or HTML if you format the text of an e-mail. Some files can't be opened by your recipient. (Text-only and RichText Format attachments are usually safe.)

Use plenty of line breaks. A large block of solid text in an e-mail looks horrible and is hard to read.

If your e-mail has two or three topics, use two or three headlines—even if each topic is only one paragraph. Signal headlines by adding a line break, or adding a line of a keyboard character such as ~, ^, *. - or =.

Example:
~~~~~~

Why use special characters to signal headings? Well, you can certainly insert bold and larger fonts into your e-mail, but will they still be there at the other end? You can't control the way your correspondent views your e-mail. It may arrive as plain text or with gobbledegook or HTML. The system above is the safe way.

Don't use SOLID CAPS except for headings. Solid caps are regarded as shouting on the Internet, which is considered rude.

Etiquette for an e-mail list

Do you receive messages that go to many people on an e-mail list? Here's how you can help an e-mail list run smoothly.

Do these things.

1. If you want to reply to one particular person, and not to everyone else on the list as well, type that person's e-mail address in the 'to' section up top. (If you just hit 'reply', everyone on the list will get your message.)

2. Use a new and accurate subject line when you reply.

3. Retain the vertical line or the quote marks (>>>) that indicate you are quoting from an earlier message. And delete all irrelevant parts of the earlier message.

4. Keep the format absolutely simple. Use the same standard font throughout.

5. If you can't decipher a message from the list, say so.

6. Be nice to all newbies, or others may become too scared to contribute.

Don't do these things.

1. Don't click on 'Reply' unless you really do want your reply to go to everyone else on the list. (See #1 on the 'Do' list above.)

2. Don't assume everyone has the latest software: keep things very simple.

3. Don't indulge in pointless chatter.
~~~~~~

4. Don't attach a file if you can avoid it. Put the information in the body of the e-mail.

5. Don't forward a message that includes an attachment. Most lists cannot cope with this. Instead, send a brand new message to the list with the attachment.

6. Don't send personal messages to the list.

7. Don't type anything in solid caps. That's considered rude.

8. Don't provide two e-mail addresses because then you'll receive every message twice.

9. Don't discuss fees and prices with others on the list.

10. Don't forward other people's e-mails to outsiders unless you get permission first.

Writing faxes

Treat a fax just like a memo, except that:

- your reader is usually in an external office (not in your own building)
- a fax is usually addressed to just one person.

Sending and receiving faxes used to be a big deal. Some early fax sheets had huge headings. They even shouted in pride and awe—'It's a fax!!!!' You needed a special black pen to communicate. But we don't need all this excitement now.

Today, most offices have faxes, though their role is largely being overtaken by e-mail. If international clients communicate to you by fax, reply by fax. Faxes may be their most reliable communication technology.

Make sure your stationery signals that this is a fax, not a memo or a letter. (It won't always be obvious, because some fax machines use normal paper.) Clearly show your return fax number. That's the main thing your correspondent will need when replying. (The print-out at the top of the page may include your fax number, but it's often blurred.)

As with an e-mail or letter, put as much detail as possible in your subject line. Then the fax can be handed straight to the right person.

Essential details in a fax heading

(*your logo*)

Fax from.......................................Fax number.......................................

Fax to..Fax number......................................

Date...Number of pages (incl. this)...............

Subject...

(*message follows*)

Writing memos

A memo is just a letter without an envelope. It's sent to a number of people—or sometimes just one person—within the same organisation. Follow the guidelines for letters.

The format is usually standardised, which saves time for you and the reader.

Typical memo format

(*your logo*)

Memo
to...

Memo
from...Phone...................................

Subject...Date.........................

Action
required..

(*contents of memo follows*)

Writing letters

Remember the first rule of plain English: put the needs of the reader first. When you read a letter, what do you want to know—quickly?

1. Who is this letter from?

2. What's it about? Is it good news or bad news?

3. What do they want me to do?

4. Do I have to read the whole thing?

The secret of writing good business letters is to provide answers to all the above questions—quickly.

Who is this letter from?

That's the easy bit. Your business letter carries the company letterhead. It's obvious who the letter is from. Besides, you sign it.

What's this letter about?

As a general rule, tell your reader immediately what the letter is about. Use a bold subject line (directly after the hello-phrase). Pack the essential information into the subject line.

PLAIN	Your stationery order #3999 despatched 3 May 1999
UNCLEAR	Order #3999

The subject line prepares your readers, helping them to grasp your key message quickly. The subject line is for the benefit of your reader. It will also make filing easier for both sender and receiver—but that's just a bonus.

Don't use 'RE.' at the start of your subject line. 'RE.' is a redundant hangover from the days of the typewriter. 'Re' means 'about a thing'—in other words, 'this letter is about this thing'. But today we use bold, which automatically signals the function of the subject line.

(With bad news letters, or persuasive letters, you may decide to use a more discreet or vague subject line, or drop it altogether.)

What do they want me to do?

Many business letters require the receiver to do something—send a cheque, confirm a postal address, answer a question, fill in a form. Tell readers exactly what you want them to do, preferably in the very first or second sentence. Say 'you' and 'I' and 'we'. Then readers can quickly see what they need to do. 'Please' is a godsend for this important section of your letter.

Do I have to read the whole thing?

Think about what happens when you read a business letter. Many times, you'll stop reading after the first couple of paragraphs, and just glance at the remainder. This is now a convention: people simply assume that the most important part of the letter is at the top.

You can't force people to read every word you write, so make sure:

- your letter is as short as possible
- your subject line is clear, complete and descriptive
- you tell readers immediately what you want them to do
- the most important material is at the top of the letter
- nothing important is buried in the middle or at the end.

The audit-trail sentence

Your audit-trail sentence reminds the reader what happened last. If this is an ongoing correspondence, start with a very short sentence such as these:

PLAIN Thank you for your inquiry of 3 June 2000.
I'm replying to your letter of 10 September 1999.
I'd like to confirm in writing what we agreed by telephone yesterday.

State only one idea in this short opening sentence.

Don't try to compress your audit-trail-sentence into a single phrase. For example, don't start like this:

FANCY Further to your recent letter explaining why your final income tax payment was delayed, ...

FANCY In response to your inquiry about whether scarlet feathers are available...

If you start a sentence this way, you might die before you finish it. Many people waste precious time over their audit-trail sentence. They start with a clichéd phrase and find the sentence goes on and on and on, getting more and more tangled along the way. Cut to the chase: just say 'Thank you...'

Punctuating addresses

Omit punctuation in addresses. Many postal sorting machines cannot read addresses that include commas, hyphens or periods. For this reason, an envelope with punctuation in the address may take longer to arrive.

Make an exception when writing to non-English speaking countries. In these cases, copy the exact address and punctuation from your correspondent's stationery.

The hello phrase (or salutation)

You'll save time using a modern salutation! No more dithering over whether to say 'Ms' or 'Mrs' or 'Mr'.

Today, you don't need to write 'Mr', 'Miss', 'Mrs' or 'Ms' to people in English-speaking countries. But some titles such as 'Dr' and 'Professor' are perceived as important, so include them at least in letters to people you don't know. When writing to non-English speaking people, determine the person's exact title and always use it.

Direct marketing letters omit the Miss/Ms/Mrs/Mr tag with no ill effects.

> Elisa Falisiu
> HR Manager
> Elexitronics Ltd
> 23 Bristol Street
> Epping NSW 2121
>
> Dear Elisa Falisiu
>
> *(subject line or start of text)*

Notice that a comma after 'Elisa Falisiu' is not necessary. However, that comma is still quite common in North America and Europe.

How about using only the personal name, starting with 'Dear Bob' or just 'Bob'? No problem if you know the person. But should you use only a personal name when you don't know the person? That largely depends on how traditional your company guidelines are. Modern practice in the English-speaking world is increasingly to use personal names—even with people you don't know. However, this assumed intimacy may still offend some people.

Is 'Dear' necessary? Actually, no—not in the modern world! If you want to, just drop it. Albert Joseph, author of *Put it in Writing!*[7] says he has not

[7] ISBN 0-07-039308-7

used 'Dear' in a letter in over two decades. He says that very few people even notice, and others regard it as unimportant. Most people you write to in business are not dear to you. And the word 'Dear' does nothing to soften an unwelcome message.

If you know the person you're writing to, or if your company uses the more casual, modern approach, it's acceptable to streamline the address and salutation like this:

Alex Kedgeley
HR Manager
Elexitronics Ltd
98 Lapis Grove
East Maitland 2323
Australia

Alex

(subject line)

Again, a comma after 'Alex' is not necessary.

How about when you really cannot find out the name of the person? Or when it's not appropriate to spend time identifying the person? Write to the organisation. That is fine, and has been for the past twenty years.

PLAIN Dear Inland Revenue Department
PLAIN Dear Maritime Safety Authority of Switzerland

And by the way, you'd never start a letter with 'Dear Sir or Madam'—would you? This reeks of the nineteenth century when business people (the mere middle classes) grovelled to the upper classes, who never paid their bills anyway. Recently I even received an e-mail from a client signed 'Esq.'

How about the modern goodbye phrase? If you're over 40, forget what you learned at school: 'Yours faithfully' is regarded as old-fashioned. 'Yours sincerely' 'Sincerely' or 'Kind regards' is fine for both formal and informal letters. No need for a comma or period. (Actually, when you think about it, even 'Yours sincerely' is a little absurd. The writer probably is sincere—but I'm not yours and you're not mine!)

In New Zealand, a Maori salutation is sometimes appropriate. Instead of 'Dear so-and-so', you can start a formal letter:

- Tena koe, Hone (*to one person*)
- Tena korua, Hone and Janetta (*to two people*)
- Tena koutou, Hone, Janetta and Huia (*to three or more people*)
- Kia ora (*informal*).

To complete the Maori salutations, end a formal letter with 'Kati ake nei, Hei kona mai'. And you can end an informal letter with 'Ka kite ano'.

Most news/bad news structure

The structure of a letter with good news or neutral information is pretty foolproof. Stick tight to the following order unless you have an extremely good reason for deviating from it:

1. exact subject (stated in the subject line)
2. audit-trail sentence (if appropriate)
3. the main point: who, what, where, when, how
4. action required
5. additional information if any.

The structure outlined above is called the inverted pyramid because the big message is at the top. It's essential for news stories and Web pages, and it's normal practice in business English.

By contrast, the traditional 'bad news' letter inserts the bad news in paragraph four, like the meat in a sandwich. First you prepare the reader for the bad news, then you deliver the bad news, then you suggest a way of moving on from the bad news.

Conventional structure of a bad news letter

1. 'Thank you for applying/explaining/writing... I understand...'
   In paragraph #1, show that you have considered the person/application/complaint seriously, and that you empathise.

2. In paragraph #2, give reasons for the decision based on policy or the general situation. Show that the rejection is not personal.

3. Give the bad news in paragraph #3. State it very clearly—once only. Don't apologise. Don't say 'unfortunately'. You mean it kindly but this doesn't help. In fact, it can make matters worse.

4. Finally, suggest actions the reader could take or ways of moving on OR wish the person well in their job-hunt/business/whatever. (End on a positive note.)

The above structure doesn't necessarily suit every situation or every reader. In some cases, the reader only wants to know whether the answer is 'yes' or 'no. Then the letter should be very short. Courteous, correct—but short. Long explanations may be seen as insincere, a waste of time, or even insulting.

When you must write a bad news letter, judge each situation on its own merits. If you can, consult colleagues, because such letters are hard to write. When it comes to the point, all bad news letters are just that—bad news. You can't turn it into good news, no matter how you grovel.

Sometimes you must write a letter of apology. Apologise only once, but do it properly. Make your apology whole-hearted and complete. Don't hedge it with ifs and buts. Explain exactly how you will make amends or prevent the offence from occurring again.

Letters containing complex information

If you must convey a lot of information or complex information in one letter, you need to break it up somehow. Follow the inverted pyramid structure, putting the essential point right up front. Separate the other topics, and give them their own headings. Thus a letter might have a subject line (which refers to the whole letter) and two or three sub-headings introducing the other points.

In these cases, you have even more reason to write concisely. Try to limit the letter to two pages.

Sales letters

With direct marketing letters, assume all your readers will be strongly resistant. You have to grab their attention in the first sentence.

Starting with a pertinent question works well. Example:

How can you stop this flow of unwanted, anonymous e-mails?

Use ultra-plain English consistently. Sentences of 10-16 words. Very short, strong, punchy verbs. 'You' throughout. Contractions such as 'you'll', 'you've' etc. Paragraphs of 1-3 sentences.

Use positive language:

1. Stress what something is rather than what it is not.

2. Emphasize what the firm or product can and will do.

3. Open with action, never with an apology or explanation.

4. Avoid negative words and words that convey unpleasant feelings.

At the end of the letter, press for action. For example, 'Sign here', 'Ring this 0800 number', 'Use the self-addressed envelope'. Without this, your efforts are wasted.

They say the right headline can increase your response rate by up to 1700%! Of course there's no such thing as 1700%, but you get the picture. There's a huge difference between a headline that is merely OK and one that penetrates to the heart of your reader's needs.

Dramatise! Describe a specific situation—be there beside your customers. See what they see, sense what they sense.

> You know you're home when you see the vivid yellow of Scentasia roses beside your front door and smell their delicate citron perfume.
>
> If you want to drink just one glass of your favourite wine, fine! Use the Vacuumcork and drink the rest the following day. It'll still be perfect.

And use the power of the PS. Put something significant in the PS—the guarantee or the 'save $100 by applying today' sentence. People usually read the PS even if they skip the body of the letter.

(More about persuasive writing in Chapter 5.)

Letters to international clients

You may be corresponding with people from non-English speaking countries. Your international clients have their own courtesy conventions. Take their cue. In general, be more formal. Use 'Dear' and always use the correct titles.

Write simply. Use short sentences. Your letter or fax is likely to be read by many people, including some whose English is minimal.

You may need to structure letters differently in international correspondence. If your Japanese or Mexican clients begin letters by asking after your family or commenting on seasonal changes, respond the same way. If your Russian clients state their message bluntly, be equally blunt.

Separate courtesy paragraphs from business. Never try and write 'more politely'—you'll probably become incomprehensible. Instead, dedicate a few sentences to building the relationship, and put them at the beginning and end of the letter. And always write in short sentences. A long, difficult sentence can make you seem arrogant or shifty, as if you are choosing to be obscure.

Global English for Global Business[8] gives comprehensive guidelines on successful international communication. It is essential reading if you do business with countries that don't have English as their first language.

Write letters the easy way

Many people feel insecure about writing letters. But it's easy if you just:

1. write down what you'd say if your reader was in the room with you
2. then fix what you wrote.

What do I mean by 'fix'? For details, see Chapter 9. In brief, you:

- check that items are in the best order for the reader
- check that you've covered everything
- cut out unnecessary words, sentences and paragraphs
- check and correct the content, grammar and punctuation.

Using this simple process, you'll write letters faster and more confidently. You'll just say what you mean—simply and clearly. You won't suffer the strain of writing fancy, old-fashioned, formal, wordy prose.

Naturally, you'll write all your letters in plain English. Anything else can damage your company profile, and is actively wasting time and money.

---

[8] © Rachel McAlpine 1997. ISBN 0-582-73998-5

Portrait of a modern business letter

Clear (not unclear, obscure or muddled)
Concise (saying a lot in few words)
Conversational (not fancy or literary)
Complete (including all necessary information)
Courteous (not cold or rude)
Concrete (specific, not vague and waffly)
Constructive (leading to some action; positive)
Correct (in grammar, punctuation, facts and format)

Stop when you're through

When you've said what you need to say in a letter, stop. The following awful cliché is far too common.

FANCY Should you have any queries, please do not hesitate to call the writer on 095 776 3490.

'What's wrong with that?' you ask.

- It's old-fashioned ('Should...').
- It's a double negative ('do not hesitate').
- It's impersonal ('the writer').
- It implies a crazy scenario.[9]
- And it's a cliché.

People rarely read that last sentence. (Do you, honestly?) Certainly, the thought is better when expressed in plain English.

PLAIN Please call me if you have any questions.

Even so, think twice about ending this way—don't do it automatically. Do you sincerely mean this invitation? Concentrate on making your letter perfectly clear to readers. Then they won't need to phone you.

---

[9] Your reader thinks of calling you. She hesitates. Then she remembers you told her not to hesitate. Too late! Now what? (And does she care?)

Write a media release

Free publicity is yours for the asking! If you write a good press release you're half way there... but you have to do it right.

Nothing is news just because you say so. Make it newsworthy. Identify one main point that will interest the public. By definition, news is new, news is topical, and news affects people.

Will they print it?

An editor may publish your media release exactly the way it is, or change it, or ignore it completely. By doing everything right you give your media release the best possible chance of being published. But be aware that on the day, there may not be room for your story about a new product. It's humbling, but war stories always take precedence.

What's your angle? What will interest people about this piece of news? Does your news concern a famous person? A scientific breakthrough? A new trend? Is there an unusual or controversial aspect of this news?

Write a media release just like a news item in the newspaper. Keep focused on the newsworthy angle. Keep it simple: short words, short sentences. Plain English is compulsory.

Start by giving the story in a one-sentence nutshell. That sentence should tell who, what, when and where. Focus on your 'angle'. Adhere strictly to the inverted pyramid structure: after the beginning, every paragraph must be less important than the one before. Editors can then remove your final paragraphs without spoiling the story or having to rewrite.

Write a headline that says who did what. Make it active and happening now. Examples:

> Philosopher destroys scones
> Y3K software sells 20 squillion

Use wide margins and a standard font. If you're sending the media release by fax or mail, follow the conventions below.

Standard media release format

MEDIA RELEASE

For immediate release/for release after (*date*)
17 March 1998 (*date)*
Joan Erikssen (*your name*)
Phone 021 123 456 (*your day-and-night phone number*)

Headline: **Nursery Rhymes Teach Children Math**
(*main text goes here*)
(*this signals the end of the text*)

CONTACT
Joan Erikssen
McKenzie, McKenzie & McKenzie
Phone 021 123 456 day or night
joane@compuserve.com

Photo attached (*protect it with cardboard*)
Photo and video opportunity: (*place, time, date)*

If you're posting the media release on a Web site, change the format so that the text starts with something meaningful (not your personal name, title and phone number). Otherwise search results will probably show garbage instead of real content. At the top, put only the company name. Put your own name, e-mail and day-and-night phone number at the bottom.

Do your homework: target specific journalists by name. Never deal with more than one person in the same magazine, newspaper, TV or radio station. That causes confusion and severe annoyance. Always contact the same person, and build a good working relationship.

Send press releases by mail, if non-urgent, or by e-mail. Faxes are usually third choice because most faxes are flimsy and self destruct.

Know the deadlines of publications, and TV and radio shows. Send your media release well before the event. Call in advance to say a media release is on its way. Send another media release later as a reminder. Answer journalists' calls immediately: they have deadlines, and old news is no news.

4

Reports

Inform, interpret, advise

Whatever your job title, you are likely to write reports from time to time. Make sure your reports are clear, complete and correct. They are often the main way in which you communicate with your clients.

Basically, in a report you relate what happened—who did what, when, where, how, why—and how you interpret these events. Some reports are analytical. Some reports recommend actions.

Remember the number one rule of plain English: write for your reader!

This chapter explains how to:

1. think before you start writing a report
2. clarify the purpose and scope of a report
3. streamline the process of writing reports
4. include the essential parts of a report
5. make sure each section does its duty
6. structure reports for the reader's convenience
7. write the all-important executive summary
8. select a report style: conservative, modern, or a happy compromise.

Think first!

When writing even a short report, be very sure you know:

- Who asked you to write this report?
- Exactly what were you asked to do?
- What is the purpose of this report?
- Who is your primary audience?
- Who else will read this report?

Who asked you to write this report? You don't just write a report because you feel like it. Normally someone requests you to write one. This could be your boss, your manager or a client. In some cases, writing reports is a requirement of your job.

Exactly what were you asked or required to do? Clarify the purpose and scope of the report. What are your terms of reference? Were you asked to spend a week or a year on this report? To simply survey the situation—or to investigate, analyse and make recommendations? To consult with experts, to run experiments, or just to do research using books, journals and the Internet? To report in person, by e-mail or in hard copy?

Never be satisfied by the brief you are given at first. Verify your terms of reference, and be very sure about the scope. Don't skimp on the time you spend on this, but regard it as an essential part of writing a report, which will ultimately save you time, money and frustration.

Read your instructions carefully. Think about the implications. Then phone or visit the person who gave you your brief. Ask questions. Listen.

Nine times out of ten this exercise brings interesting results. The brief is clarified or even alters as you discuss it with the person concerned.

How long should your report be? Reports vary greatly in length:

- a single paragraph (e.g. an incident report)
- one or two pages (e.g. a letter report)
- 30 pages (e.g. an Annual Report)
- hundreds of pages (e.g. a report on a five-year investigation).

What is the purpose of this report? Is it just for the record? Is the purpose to assist a client to develop a business? To advise management on policy? To influence government? To solve a particular problem? To fulfil tax requirements? To confirm to sponsors that their money was well-spent? To highlight problems without attempting to solve them?

Have the purpose clear in your mind from the word go. In fact, write it down, because this will help you keep on track.

This report updates...
surveys...
recommends changes to...
analyses...
provides information about...
explains the benefits of...
alerts...

Who is your primary audience? They may or may not be the same person who asked you to write the report. Keep the intended readers always in your mind. How much do they know already? What do they need to know? What questions will they ask? What's most important to them?

Who else will read this report? Often a report will be read by many people. For example, you may write a report for a non-technical manager, but it may also be read by board members, managers in other departments, the media, technical experts and the general public.

It's a challenge to satisfy all these various needs. You can do so by using plain English, and by structuring your report intelligently.

The process of report writing

So much to write—so little time—so much at stake! When you have to write a long report the task can seem overwhelming.

The process has several stages. The following strategies will help you to write quickly and keep control of your material.

1. Think first. Be clear about audience, purpose, brief and scope.

2. Gather information. Brainstorm. Consult. Keep records, references and files in good order.

3. Analyse and sort material. Select material, keeping the purpose and scope in mind.

4. Outline the report. What content is essential, what is unnecessary? Organise material into sections and subsections. Arrange sections in the best order. Write headings for each. Up to this point, use phrases only—never start writing sentences till you've outlined the report, because it's a waste of time.

5. Start writing a rough draft, in sentences. Start anywhere. Use plain English. Write as you would talk. Write rapidly, don't edit, and don't worry about errors. (You'll fix them later.)

6. Prepare graphics.

7. Write the executive summary—the most important part of your report.

8. Get feedback from colleagues. Revise rough draft in three stages. (i) Check content—is it complete? Valid? Relevant to purpose and reader? Are graphics apt and necessary? (ii) Does it flow smoothly? In logical order? (iii) Correct style, punctuation, grammar.

Usual sections of a report

Every report must include certain essential sections. The sections may be in any order. They may have more descriptive names, but they must be in the report somewhere. Other sections on the list below are optional; include them if they are in your brief. (A long report may have other sections also.)

1. ESSENTIAL: Title page

2. ESSENTIAL: Table of contents

3. ESSENTIAL: Executive summary

4. ESSENTIAL: Introduction (brief, purpose, scope, limitations)

5. OPTIONAL: Background (may be a special section, or included in the introduction, or an appendix)

6. ESSENTIAL: Conclusions

7. OPTIONAL: Recommendations

8. OPTIONAL: Costs

9. OPTIONAL: Methods

10. ESSENTIAL: Body/discussion

11. OPTIONAL: Conclusion

12. OPTIONAL: Appendixes[10]

---

[10] Appendixes and appendices are both correct plurals of appendix. I suggest you take the easy option.

Make each section do its duty

Title page

The title page is a powerful tool. Make it work hard! The title itself can summarise your report's main findings. Try using a creative title plus a descriptive subtitle, or vice versa. Start with a keyword or key phrase, highly relevant to your topic. Not 'Report on...' or 'Study of...' Get to the point! A clever title page foreshadows or summarises the entire report.

Table of contents

A table of contents is essential for any report longer than two or three pages. It acts as a preview or roadmap for the reader. It tells readers what to expect and shows the structure of your report. In other words, it prepares the reader to read efficiently.

Executive summary

Every report should begin with an executive summary, which must summarise the entire report in ordinary, readable language. In less than one page, summarise your brief, the background, your conclusions, your recommendations and the discussion.

After reading the executive summary, the reader should have a grip of all your main points. A proper executive summary empowers readers and gives them confidence that your report is orderly, complete and well written.

Even very short reports should start with a paragraph or sentence that makes the main point. (More about the executive summary later.)

Introduction and methods

A good introduction states the precise subject of the report, the reasons for the report, and perhaps the way the report is organised. In 100-300 words, it focuses the reader's attention. Style should be clear and interesting.

In your introduction you must:

- state the original terms of reference (who asked you to do what)[11]
- state the purpose of the report
- state the scope (and limitations, if any) of the report.

---

[11] Often called the 'brief'.

The introduction may also discuss the background—the prevailing situation, or history, or problem, or context of the report. Always ask yourself, 'Does my primary reader need to know this?' If not, omit the background material or put it in an appendix. On the other hand, if the background is highly significant and requires a page or more, create a special Background section.

You may describe your methodology in the introduction. But if your methods form a major part of the report, make that a separate section.

Conclusions

The conclusions section must summarise what you have discovered, realised, concluded or deduced as a result of your investigations. You must state your conclusions—usually in a dedicated section. Some people read only this section, so it should make sense alone. Stress the most significant points.

Your 'Conclusions' have nothing to do with concluding the report, so they're not usually placed at the end.

Recommendations

Often your brief includes recommending a course of action. If so, you must obviously include your recommendations in the report. If possible (and if this fits your brief) be specific: say exactly who should do exactly what, and in what order. Do not write airy-fairy recommendations such as, 'That there should be world peace.'

Cost/Comparative costs/Estimate of costs

If you're recommending a course of action, or comparing several different courses of action, your readers will be very, very, very interested in the probable or definite cost. Tell them.

Body/Discussion

The substance of your report is here. Expect this to be the longest part of your report. Make the body of your report user-friendly by subdividing it into smaller parts. Use plenty of explanatory headings. Always keep your main readers in mind. What do they need to know first? most? last? least? Base your decisions about order and structure on the readers' needs.

Conclusion

A conclusion section rounds off the entire report. Its purpose is to remind people of the main points in the report. It's not necessary in a short paper, although it is quite a pleasant thing to add.

Appendixes

In some reports you need to incorporate extra bits and pieces. You might want to include background material, technical details, large tables or flow charts. Include these extra items last as appendixes. Label them (Appendix A, Appendix B) and also give each one a title.

Structure reports for the reader's convenience

Structure is perhaps your most powerful tool for helping the reader absorb and understand your report. Five structural devices will help you get your message across.

1. Tell them what you're going to tell them, then tell them, then tell them what you've told them. Your main point can be made on the title page, and in the executive summary and again in the body or discussion or conclusions.

2. Ask yourself what the reader wants to know most urgently. Put those points at the beginning. (You're not writing a mystery novel.) Often that means starting the report this way: (i) Executive summary (ii) Recommendations (iii) Cost.

3. Start every report with an executive summary. Then your lucky reader can get the gist of the entire report before reading the rest (or scanning the rest or ignoring the rest).

4. Use descriptive, specific, interesting headings that summarise the following sections.

5. Use graphics where appropriate.

The all-important executive summary

What's an executive summary? It is a condensed version of the entire report. It's a précis, a synopsis, a short, predigested version of the report. Sometimes it's called simply a summary or an overview. The executive summary:

- is usually about 200-300 words (one page maximum)
- covers every important aspect of the report, including purpose, methods, recommendations and cost
- is easy and interesting to read
- mentions items in the same order as they occur in the report
- is preferably in straight prose (without bullet points).

Confusion about the executive summary is widespread. The executive summary:

- is not a hotch-potch of text cobbled together from the report
- is not a selection of points from the report
- is not an abstract (abstract style: 'This report discusses...')
- is not an introduction or background.

The executive summary works only if it summarises all the main points in the report. Anything less can cause dangerous confusion, as executive officers may miss some critical point. Anything less can irritate people who would then feel forced to read the entire report. Many people will read the executive summary and nothing but the executive summary—that's what it's for! Therefore, you must summarise every section.

Note that an executive summary is not an abstract. An abstract is very brief—perhaps 50 words—and summarises only the purpose, scope and major findings of a report. Abstracts are used by libraries to index academic and scientific reports. Abstracts are by definition dry and objective, whereas an executive summary should be interesting to read.

Why is an executive summary necessary?

The word 'executive' implies the following scenario.

An executive officer is about to attend a meeting at which your report will be discussed. He's been too busy to read the report. He stops by your desk and asks for a rapid summary of the main points—in one minute flat. After your masterly, interesting, concise and accurate summary, the executive strides into the meeting, prepared to discuss the report with confidence.

Reports are frequently read by different people for different purposes. Technical parts of the report are irrelevant to most of your readers, but essential reading for technicians and quality control officers. Your cost analysis will be examined in detail by accountants but merely scanned by HR staff. Your appendix on the background may be of great interest to the media but painfully familiar to your colleagues.

However, every one of your intended readers must be able to read the executive summary and understand it.

When and how do you write the executive summary?

Write it last. When the report is finished and every detail is fresh in your head, sit down and write the executive summary.

Start from scratch. Don't even think about cutting and pasting bits of the report together.

Think about that executive-in-a-hurry. 'What's this all about? Quick!' Talk to the executive on paper. Write quickly. Say what the report's about, why you wrote it, what your findings are, what actions you recommend and how much they'll cost. Some people find a tape recorder useful here.

When you've written a rough draft in a natural, conversational tone, edit the draft into plain English. (See Chapter 9.)

Use graphics for facts and figures

Use visual methods to make your point where possible. A well-designed, perfectly captioned table, pie chart, bar graph, line graph or photograph is worth a thousand words. But make sure your graphics are appropriate, simple, necessary, and clearly captioned. Favour captions that explain rather than simply label.

Provide data only once. Put figures either in a graphic or table, or in the text—never both. Insert the graphics straight after the first mention of this information in the text, or with other figures at the end of the section.

Line graphs (also called line charts). Line graphs are useful, familiar, and extremely common. Use them to show changes over time, or to show the interaction of two variables over time. Make them simple and clear, preferably with only 1-4 lines. The variables must be continuous.

Show the amount on the vertical axis and show time on the horizontal axis.

Fig 1. Sales: Hinds

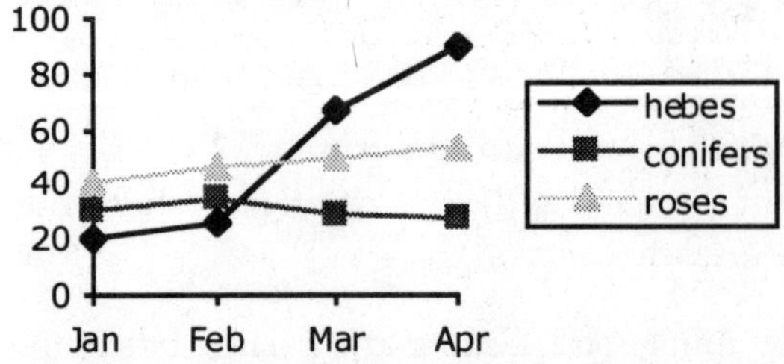

Surface charts are similar, except that all the lines add up, so the top line is the total of all the other lines. Use a surface chart to show changes in how a variable is composed.

Fig 2. Sales: Dunedin

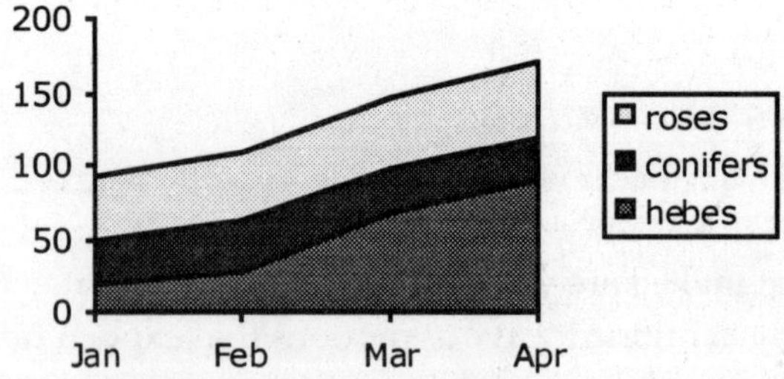

Bar graphs. Bar charts are useful and versatile—they are nearly as common as line graphs in annual reports. They can be used for a wide range of information. Limit the number and types of bars so they clearly convey the information.

Bar graphs can be vertical or horizontal. They can start from a base line or go in two directions from a mid-line, showing both positive and negative quantities.

Fig 3. Sales: Belfast

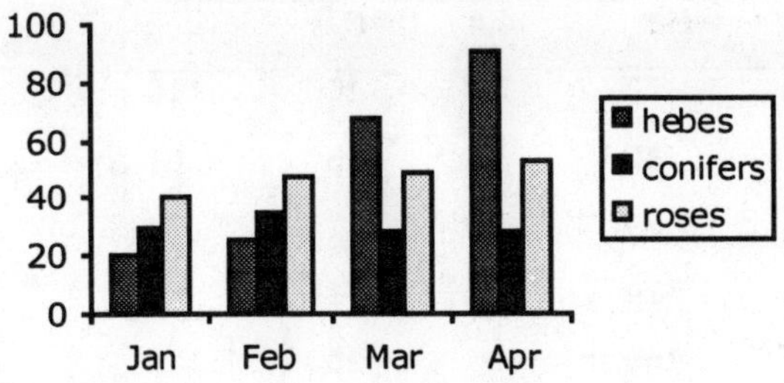

Pie charts. Again, keep them simple. If you have more than 6 sections, a pie chart loses impact. (A section called 'other' can solve this problem.)

Pie charts show the composition of the whole. Label each section clearly. There's usually plenty of room for labels around a pie chart.Always show percentages of the whole, and make sure they add up to 100%. Sometimes you will also put the exact figure.

Commonly, the biggest section of pie is at the 12 o'clock position, and other sections are arranged in some logical order.

Fig 4. 1999 sales Hinds

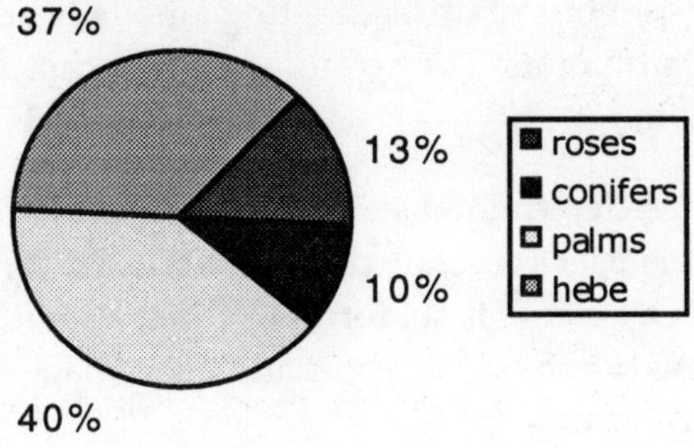

Tables: these show data in a highly concentrated form, so use them only when absolutely necessary. Keep tables as brief and simple as possible. Don't put whole sentences in cells. Put numbers to be compared in adjacent columns. Put like elements across in rows, and unlike elements vertically in columns.

Fig 5. 1999 sales: Akaroa

	Jan	Feb	Mar	Apr	May	June
hebes	20	26	67	90	100	110
roses	41	47	49	53	50	61
conifers	30	35	29	28	25	33
palms	12	19	24	22	15	13
TOTAL	103	127	169	193	190	217

Choose your report format: traditional or modern?

Today there's a tug-of-war between champions of the traditional report format and champions of the modern format.

RULE #1. Follow your company style guide.

If your company or organisation has a set format for reports, use it. The format ordained by your company style guide takes precedence over all the advice you're reading here. (If necessary, start a campaign to modernise your old-fashioned templates.)

RULE #2. Use a modern format if you can.

Old-fashioned reports were produced on typewriters, which were severely limited. They had very few methods of differentiating among headings or drawing attention to important points. They could use block capitals and underlining, and that was about it.

In the past, all reports used predetermined sections with predetermined generic labels. Every report had sections called INTRODUCTION, BACKGROUND, DISCUSSION etc. This set format helped to guide readers through the report in the days when every report and every page looked the same. Now there are other options.

By tradition, old-fashioned reports use digital numbering for sections and subsections. Today, digital numbering nearly always seems finickity and cluttered and pointless. (It's still compulsory in much legislation.)

Example:

1. Introduction
    1.1 Purpose
        1.1.1 Exploring Intranet options
        1.1.2 Recommend browser choice
    1.2 Background
        1.2.1 History of company communication
        1.2.2 Pressures on archiving

The computer differentiates by design

Modern reports are produced on a computer. With a computer you can use:

- styles (a hierarchy of headings automatically formatted by your word processor)
- bullet points
- different fonts and font sizes
- bold and italic
- indented, justified, centred and right aligned text
- headers and footers
- graphics including tables, graphs and charts.

Readers find their way around a modern, well-designed report intuitively. Using a computer, there is rarely any advantage in numbering sections.

A modern table of contents, without decimal numbers, is user-friendly. It shows readers exactly where to find particular items. Good design signals headings and subheadings clearly, so a number like '4.4.5' in the middle of a report doesn't necessarily help the reader in any way.

Modern headings tell the story. You can be pretty certain that the readers of your report are busy busy busy people. You can help them enormously by using plenty of specific, descriptive headings. Such headings make a document easy to scan and understand.

PLAIN	(DESCRIPTIVE HEADINGS)
	Thirty-minute pizza delivery in Raglan
	Sample of 2000 smokers selected
	Non-monetary rewards for workers
UNCLEAR	(GENERIC HEADINGS)
	Background
	Methodology
	Discussion

The happy compromise format

As a happy compromise between traditional and modern formats, try this:

- do not number sections and subsections
- do use traditional generic headings ('Introduction', 'Discussion' etc.)
- add descriptive headings immediately after the generic headings.

Example:

> *Background*
> **Fifty years of split infinitives**

A compromise between traditional and modern format is particularly useful when staff members have differing opinions about the best format. (I expressed that very tactfully, didn't I?) It should also satisfy all your clients, whatever their expectations about format.

You can vary your writing style according to the level of formality required. Modern reports should generally be in plain English. However, in extremely formal reports, don't use 'you' at all, and use 'I' or 'we' only in an executive's personal message or your recommendations.

5

Proposals: persuasion in print

Proposals are not reports

A proposal is when you get down on your knees and beg someone to accept your offer. A proposal is not a written account of the results of your inquiry. That's a report. And they're different—very different.

Sure, the line between proposals and reports may blur occasionally. But generally, the job of a proposal is to persuade. It's a more passionate, more urgent document than a report.

Much is at stake when you write a proposal. When you write a report, your fee is usually guaranteed. Either the report is commissioned or you're doing it as part of your salaried work. But a proposal is frequently written on spec. Whether it generates any income depends on you. When you write an excellent proposal, you have a much better chance of winning the job.

Your potential client has a problem or a need. In a proposal, you offer a solution. You want to persuade the client to accept your solution and engage you to implement it. (You want the client's business!) Your aim is to present an irresistible case.

Unlike a report, a proposal is:

- a persuasive document
- a competitive document (when others compete for the same business)
- often, an unsolicited document for which you won't get paid.

Proposals can be as short as a one page letter, or a document inches thick. Tenders for large jobs can comprise several volumes.

Briefer is better. If your proposal is the shortest one in the pile, the decision maker will probably read your proposal first. It will immediately appear to be the most attractive, friendliest proposal—just because it's short. So don't throw in everything but the kitchen sink. Just include all the essentials.

Every proposal must be unique. You don't want your client to start muttering, 'I bet you say that to all the girls!' Focus on your client's specific business needs first, last, and right throughout the proposal. Reflect and paraphrase the client's words before you suggest a solution.

Many people hate writing proposals, because they take so much time and may produce no results. But you can speed up the process and write winning proposals using the clear guidelines and adaptable template in this book.

Responding to a Request For Tender

When you respond to an RFT you're writing a document that's a kind of proposal. Much of your tender may be purely mechanical stuff, the same for every tender. Nevertheless, study this chapter closely, because it could greatly boost your chances of success in tendering.

When tendering, your summary and covering letter should follow the guidelines in this chapter. Throughout the tender, always emphasise the client's particular needs or problem, and the benefits of your particular solution. Just a phrase or sentence here and there can make it obvious that you have the client always in mind. Clients want to know that you understand their business: that's their top priority.

This is the challenge: to streamline the process of writing proposals and responses to RFTs—and still customise every one for a particular job.

Procedures, project plans and checklists

With any large-scale proposal and with every single tender, you need foolproof systems for getting the work done.

- Procedures: who must do what, and in what order. (And at all costs, make sure your company lawyer is part of the team.)
- Flow charts or a critical path plan with deadlines for every stage.
- Technology (beyond the scope of this book).

There's no shortcut to bypass the dogged leg-work of preparing a proposal or tender. The thoroughness and quality of your document is an advertisement for the thoroughness and quality of the work you propose to do.

Think of the process as an exam: your ultimate aim is to get top of the class. For a passing grade, you absolutely must answer every single question, no matter how trivial. After meeting that basic criterion, you then have to outdo every other applicant.

What makes the difference? Who gets the contract? Success depends on whether you can demonstrate that you:

1. understand the client's business and requirements
2. have a commitment to quality
3. offer a good price and value for money
4. have a strong reputation and good references
5. are flexible about contract terms
6. have sufficient resources
7. can offer added value
8. represent a good cultural match
9. (preferably) have an existing relationship with the client.

But how do you demonstrate this? Thoroughness is not enough. Nowadays, you also need flair. The quality of your writing matters in even the most cut-and-dried tender documents. Good writing will wake your potential clients up as they open their umpteenth tender. Good writing can shove your proposal right to the head of the queue.

Persuasive structure

Your proposal or tender must convince the client that you will be good to work with. You and your company will be judged by the quality of your proposal. Therefore every proposal must show that you are someone who listens and understands, a clear thinker, a clear communicator, and well organised. You can do all this purely by the way you structure your proposal.

Create a hard-working title page and a user-friendly table of contents for any proposal more than a few pages long. Start with an executive summary. (See Chapter 4.) And regardless of the length of the proposal, use descriptive subheadings liberally.

Follow the tips in this chapter, and model your proposal on the template for proposals in Chapter 11. Then your client will subconsciously note and appreciate your well-organised, thoughtful approach.

Above all, follow the first rule of plain English—take your reader's point of view, and write for the reader's benefit. Organise the contents of your proposal on this basis: what does your reader want to know first, most, least and last? What order is right for this client?

The inverted pyramid structure is ideal for most business documents, but it's not quite right for proposals. That's because a proposal is a persuasive document. (With the inverted pyramid, remember, you sock people with the key message first, then move on to less important matters.)

Now, the underlying key message of your proposal may be, 'We can solve your particular problem with this particular solution.' But this is not always what readers want to hear first! With a proposal, you have to woo readers before you present a solution.

1. First, clients want to know that you are a good listener and you understand their business. So prove that first. Talk first about their particular company and the issues they face.

2. Secondly, they usually want to know the solution you suggest. So describe your solution second.

3. Next, they'll want to know what the benefits are to them. Place those third, along with significant facts about your product or service.

4. After being convinced that your solution is worth considering, they want to know how much it will cost. Tell them. Cost will usually be a major factor when clients are considering whether to accept your proposal. Break down costs in detail.

5. Your readers need to know exactly what they're gaining in return for their money. Is it worth spending this money? Do a cost-benefit analysis to show the payback for investing in your solution. Show the big picture.

6. Your readers want to know whether you can do what you say what you can do—so convince them. Tell them what distinguishes you from your competitors. Be specific: it's no good just asserting you're 'the best'. Use testimonials and case histories for support here.

7. At some point, either here or earlier, they'll want to know how your solution will be implemented. What methods will you use? What staff and equipment will be necessary?

8. Close by asking for the contract—again.

Anticipate objections before you write. What questions or doubts will the client raise? Answer them directly in your proposal.

Does your solution have intrinsic problems or limitations? It's best to acknowledge these in your proposal.

Double-check the so-what factor. When you've finished your first draft, scrutinise it brutally. Is there any place where your client might say, 'So what?' If so, either remove that part or explain exactly how it's relevant to your client.

Finally, in your last paragraph, ask for the contract. Make a direct and clear request for this business. Don't be passive or you could be overlooked. Ask for the contract in your proposal at least twice—once in the executive summary and once at the end of the proposal.

How to persuade your reader

People are persuaded in print by three things:

- the benefits to themselves
- facts
- testimonials from your other clients or customers.

This has now been well proven a million times over. (Maybe I exaggerate.)

Chapter 3 includes tips on writing sales letters, with advice about persuading through benefits and facts. In a proposal you can go further: persuade with case histories and testimonials. Nothing is more convincing than affirmation from your other clients.

Think about it. If a recruitment company asserts that they can increase your profits and reduce staff turnaround, this is certainly an attractive thought. But the following is much more likely to positively influence opinion:

> 'Exeseek reduced our staff turnaround from 34% to 7% in a single year, and increased the hotel's profit by 26%.' Monty Blanco, Manager, Bay Hotel, New York.

Start gathering testimonials right now for use in future proposals. Ask your clients to write a brief and very specific statement about how you have helped them. Ask them if you can quote them, complete with their name and address. Thank them, and reward them in some appropriate way.

For particular proposals, think about similar clients with similar problems that you have helped in the past. Tell the story of your big success. Discuss aspects of the case that are most relevant to your current proposal. Give the story the angle that will mean the most to the reader of this proposal.

Your covering letter

Even a one-page proposal is best sent with a short covering letter. Write it with great care. If it's boring or if it seems like a standard letter (and people can always tell), your precious proposal won't be taken seriously.

In a concise, courteous and positive way, summarise your understanding of the potential client's challenge. Give key reasons why you should be first choice, and state what you're going to do next. Ask for their business!

6

Policy, procedures and instructions

Company policy, procedures and instructions

Most organisations need to produce at least some of the following:

- policy
- written procedures
- company handbooks
- instruction manuals or reference manuals
- installation instructions
- training materials
- documentation for quality control.

Policy and procedures must be written down. That's how most disputes are settled in the workplace. Documentation ensures that procedures are formalised, and all employees receive the same instructions.

Don't let the almost random use of the words 'policy' and 'procedures' confuse you. Just be clear in your own mind about the following:

- Policies are statements of philosophy, giving an organisation's general approach to an issue. Policies may express a commitment to something like aggressive marketing or OOS prevention.
- Procedures are rules and regulations—the steps that will be taken to implement the policy.
- Instructions are literally instructions to the people who must carry out the procedures at work. 'First do this. Then do that.'

- Sometimes people use the word 'strategies' for policies or procedures. 'Strategy' implies that the organisation intends to achieve a target or reach a goal.

Good policies can keep procedures to a minimum, because when staff understand the corporate philosophy, they can judge their own actions. But policy without procedures is just wishful thinking. Procedures are the teeth of policy.

For example, a company may have a policy that forbids sexual harassment at work. But to enforce that policy, it must first set up procedures for enforcing the policy, and then tell employees what to do, step by step, if they are sexually harassed.

When writing, you generally move from policy to procedures to instructions. Vary your style accordingly.

POLICIES	PROCEDURES	INSTRUCTIONS
Cing Catering is committed to the efficient use of modern kitchen equipment.	The chef will order a new Braun food-processor every six months, and train new kitchen hands in its proper use.	1. Chop vegetables and insert in food-processor. 2. Turn on switch A. 3. Press lid down firmly. 4. Turn off switch A when processing is complete.

Pure policy

An example of policy follows. Notice the deliberately general and vague nature of the language: 'are expected to', 'should only be used', 'are not an adequate justification'. A policy does not tell people what they must do, but explains the general approach.

> **Pharmaceutical-Grade Compounds in Research**[12]
> Investigators are expected to use pharmaceutical-grade medications whenever they are available, even in acute procedures. Non-pharmaceutical-grade chemical compounds should only be used in regulated animals after specific review and approval by the IACUC for reasons such as scientific necessity or non-availability of an acceptable veterinary or human pharmaceutical-grade product. Cost savings alone are not an adequate justification for using non-pharmaceutical-grade compounds in regulated animals.

[12] Dept. of Laboratory Animal Resources at SUNY-HSC in Syracuse NY (www2.ec.hscyr.edu/dlar)

Public sector policy writing

In government, policy changes constantly. Many people are employed as full-time policy writers. If this is your job, you will probably do far more than merely record policy. You could be part of a team that actually develops public policy, based on instructions from above.

Government policy documents may be merely discussion documents, or they may outline a firm official plan for the future, or they may supply background research to a minister, or act as a discussion starter with the general public—or serve some other purpose. Therefore, members of a policy writing team must be very clear about the purpose of every policy document they write.

For example, the 'Policy and Strategy Publications' of the Department of Transport in South Africa include:

- National Policy on Airports and Airspace Management
- Report to the Minister on the 2nd Draft White Paper on the Road Accident Fund
- Road Traffic Management Strategy
- Documents for Land Transport Bills and Cross-Border Road Transport Bill.

Clearly, government policy writers have a serious responsibility. Their documents can have a significant impact on the nation. They often explore complex issues. Therefore, public policy documents must be meticulously researched, factual, realistic, and as specific as possible. (They are not persuasive documents.) Writing such documents requires a high degree of analytical skill, as well as strong communication skills.

Public sector policy style

As for style, use the rules for plain English, but modify plain English in the following ways.

Policy writers often need the passive voice. In policy, it's not usually appropriate to dictate that Somebody-Must-Do-Something. Instead, you are often stating that Something-Ought-To-Be-Done.

Policy is mostly written in the third person. It does not contain the words 'you' or 'your'.

Because many policy documents express tentative or hypothetical ideas, you need to use hypothetical verbs.

RIGHT If a subsidy for papier maché buttons were introduced, waste paper mountains would be reduced.

RIGHT Roadside goats ought to have an ample supply of grass and might require supplementary feed during winter months or drought periods.

When writing about politically sensitive topics, you may need to maintain this type of verb throughout. It's tempting to lapse into normal, forthright verbs like 'will', especially after you've written a sentence or heading that makes it obvious you are exploring a theory, not declaring a definite policy. Alas, the moment you make an assertive statement, the media or political opponents can gleefully quote that sentence out of context and imply that this policy is a fait accompli. Then all hell breaks loose. The example below demonstrates the danger—imagine the last sentence as an item on prime time news:

WRONG If a subsidy for papier maché buttons were introduced, waste paper mountains would be reduced. The consequences of this scenario could be most beneficial to the economy. Pre-school children will help their mothers to make buttons at home as a cottage industry, adding approximately $3 million to the GNP.

In policy you will often need to choose one of these helping verbs: 'will', 'would', 'should', 'could', 'can'. The most dangerous helping verb is 'should'. When someone writes, 'An arrest should be made within two days,' the author's meaning is a mystery. It has at least four possible meanings, and they're very different.

1. We expect an arrest to be made within two days, and it probably will be.
2. An arrest may possibly be made within two days—or not.
3. The police must make an arrest within two days, or there'll be trouble.
4. I advise you (the police) to make an arrest within two days.

In conversation, native English speakers usually just guess what 'should' means. But when 'should' is written, there's a high risk of miscommunication. The trouble is that 'should' can have any of the following connotations.[13]

1. DUTY. Something is obligatory, necessary, important or morally right.

2. DESIRABILITY. Something is desirable or advisable.

3. PROBABILITY. Something is likely or expected. 'One teaspoon should be enough.'

[13] Adapted from the Cambridge International Dictionary of English. ISBN 0-521-48421-9.

4. POSSIBILITY. Something possibly might happen.

5. SURPRISE. '... and who should I see but my old buddy.'

6. WOULD. 'I should like a cup of tea.'

7. ADVICE. 'I shouldn't do that if I were you' = I advise you not to do that.

8. REASON. 'Why shouldn't she buy it if she has the money?'

9. IF. (Old fashioned.) 'Should you have any queries, call me.'

EASY FIX

Often the context will make the meaning of 'should' obvious. But when in doubt, clarify the mood:

- add an adverb—for example: 'probably', 'possibly', 'preferably'
- add an adjective—for example: 'desirable', 'obligatory', 'mandatory', 'necessary', 'advisable'
- change the verb to a less ambiguous expression—for example, 'is required to', 'is legally obliged to', 'is morally bound to'.

As you see, writing public policy is tricky, and judging the correct tone is admittedly a little delicate at times. Nevertheless, there is absolutely no reason why policy documents need be written in gobbledegook. Don't let your common sense be swamped by antiquated language conventions in your workplace.

Clarity is vital. Both style and structure must be clear and user-friendly. You may be writing primarily for a minister of the crown, senator or CEO who is thoroughly conversant with the background. But such people have a stack of documents to read every day, and must not overlook any critical points. If they fail to notice some risk in the policy, their political career may suffer.

Moreover, many policy documents are also read by the public and the media. If they are incomprehensible, the government department or official lands up with egg on the face. (So do you.)

Some people will tell you in all sincerity that because a topic is complex, therefore the language must be complex. But the opposite is true: the more complex the meaning, the more important it is to write simply. Albert Einstein wrote, 'Most of the fundamental ideas of science are essentially simple and may be expressed in a language comprehensible to anyone.' The same is true of policy.

As you write, imagine a persistent, intelligent 14-year-old at your shoulder asking you again and again, 'But what do you mean?' 'I don't understand!' 'But what do you MEAN?' This imaginary teenager refuses to let you off the hook. Use language that she will understand, or else explain your jargon. Believe it, this is a great tip! This mental exercise forces you to simplify your language, and exposes any leaps or faults of logic.

On the team, be brave. Your most powerful weapon in the fight for clarity is this question: 'What does that sentence mean?' If you can't understand it (and you're on the team!) how do you expect other people to understand it?

Be particularly aggressive with abstract nouns and policy jargon. You do need such expressions when writing policy, naturally. However, when you stack a sentence with two or three abstract nouns or trendy words in a row, fog descends. In such cases, daringly insert an ordinary, familiar, concrete word such as 'people'. You may be amazed at the sudden illumination. It's like cleaning a dirty window.

Because public policy is often analytical and abstract, take particular care to use the same word for the same thing throughout. For example, don't swap from 'liquidity' to 'cash' at random: choose one or the other and stick to it. Whenever possible, choose an ordinary, familiar expression rather than a specialist term.

Policy documents must be readable by all the people they are intended for, and this often includes the general public and the media. Translate your in-house jargon into words that Joe and Joan Bloggs can understand. Use plenty of explanatory headings. Keep those sentences as short as possible. Make it easy for us all! Your purpose is to communicate, not to torture your readers.

How to write policy

In brief and in general, here's how a team tackles a policy writing job.

Stage 1

a. Clarify what this policy document is for, who asked you to write it, and who will read it.

b. Establish the scope and limitations of this document. Know exactly what content must be covered, how much detail is needed, and how long the document should be.

c. Identify the main issues.

d. Prepare an outline of the document and a provisional contents page.

e. Decide who will have responsibility for each section.

f. Decide on the layout and style of the document.

Stage 2

a. Do the research.

b. Organise your material in logically named files or one large document file in 'Outline View'.

c. Evaluate the information. (Is it true? Is it relevant? Is it important?) Select information.

d. Analyse the information. (What are the implications? What are the risks? What are the likely legal and political repercussions? What approach seems best, given all these factors?)

Stage 3

a. Write the policy document, in sections.

b. Assemble the sections and place them in the most appropriate order.

c. Re-organise the contents page.

d. Write the executive summary.

Stage 4

a. Get feedback on the draft from colleagues, legal advisers and others.

b. Modify the draft in response to feedback.

c. Get a wordsmith to edit the document into a seamless whole.

d. Check the document against your brief and legal requirements.

Stage 5

Produce the final document and distribute it.

Writing staff manuals and company handbooks[14]

A staff manual or handbook is a publication designed to communicate the organisation's work policies, rules and regulations to employees.

Employees must know what is expected of them. Clear guidelines and instructions save time and money, ensure consistent quality, and prevent industrial accidents.

Besides work rules and policies, and instructions for emergencies, the staff manual often includes:

- the company mission statement
- suggestion and complaint procedures
- employee's rights and responsibilities
- quality assurance procedures
- emergency procedures.

The staff manual is the right place for HR information about:

- performance appraisal
- personnel records
- promotions, resignations and dismissals
- benefits, pension and profit-sharing plans
- training and development opportunities
- holidays and various types of leave.

Policy, procedures and the law

Laws are constantly changing. Before the handbook is printed or goes live on the intranet, the company lawyer must check it.

Include policies and procedures that ensure compliance with legislation in all relevant areas, including:

privacy	freedom of information
fair trading	copyright
industrial relations	occupational health and safety
resource management	equal employment opportunities
employment insurance	employment contracts
affirmative action	human rights

[14] They're the same thing with different names.

Documentation requirements for ISO9001

Nowhere is the importance of good documentation more obvious than in ISO9001 requirements. Increasingly, large companies need this international acknowledgement that their quality management system (QMS) is effective. And how is your QMS defined, implemented and audited? By your documents alone! Without documentation, you don't actually have a quality management system.

Smaller companies often opt for Total Quality Management (TQM), which is similar to ISO9001, but without international registration.

Everything in this chapter and Chapter 10 is relevant to the ISO9001 Standard and to TQM. Aim for a fully computerised system with automatic reminders for every stage of documentation.

ISO9001 requires three levels of documentation:

1. The quality policy manual, usually 20 pages or fewer. It may include:
   - your company profile
   - a definition of the scope of your business and relevant activities
   - a list of all procedures that define the QMS
   - notes on how your QMS addresses each requirement of ISO9001.

2. Procedures. Usually the procedures describe the purpose of your business processes, how they are controlled, and how your controls ensure that the requirements of customers and ISO9001 are met.

3. Work instructions. You don't need instructions for everything—only where quality would otherwise be jeopardised.

7

Modern page design

'Nothing in fine print is ever good news.' Andy Rooney

The impact of the PC

The impact of the computer and word processing is immense. Older documents now seem quaint and old-fashioned. Modern documents look totally different from those that were produced by the typewriter—at least, they certainly ought to!

Design is an integral part of a plain English document. The brutal truth is that most people don't bother to read documents that are presented in a messy, crowded or confusing way. Good design encourages people to read your document, and has powerful ways of helping your reader get the message.

The personal computer means that every business, no matter how tiny, now has the tools to produce documents that are attractive and easy to read. Large corporations and organisations use professionals to produce stunning annual reports and marketing material. It wouldn't be appropriate for a sole trader to spend that much money on presentation, but even one person working from home can design documents that are balanced and easy to read. Cheap colour printers expand your possibilities further.

Now and then I teach courses at polytechnics or universities. I am appalled when students produce their assignments on old typewriters or 'word processors'—even though computers are available in the classroom. Can you believe it? This isn't poverty, it's perversity. Even an eccentric poetry editor—let alone a potential business client—will doubt the seriousness of work typed on a manual typewriter today.

Less obvious to the amateur are the pitfalls of page design. If you suspect your letters and reports look a bit klunky, cast the following tip in bronze: become hypersensitive to your own reading processes. Notice which documents you read quickly and easily, which ones you need to re-read, and which ones you can't be bothered reading. Most often the reasons lie in the design. After reading this chapter, consider those easy-to-read business letters, newsletters and annual reports with a new eye. What have they done that you could do?

An ugly letter

Intuitively you hate the look of the letter below, don't you? The rest of this chapter explains why it is ugly, and why ugly is hard to read.

> BERHAMPORE REHABILITATION CENTER
> 22 EDINBURGH TCE, WELLINGTON
>
> MR JOHN HALITIRIS,
> Top Training Team, PO Box 9999, Bulls.
>
> Dear Mr Halitiris,
> Would you please send me any brochures or information relating to programmes your company is offering this year? *I am particularly interested in training that increases employment opportunities.*
>
> Yours sincerely
> *B. A. Slough*
> B.A. Slough, Social Worker

Easy-to-read design features

Design your document for the reader's comfort. Plain English means using page design that is:

- plain—meaning simple, not fancy
- plain—meaning clear, not muddled or unclear.

Basic rules:

1. Use plenty of white space.
2. Use a standard serif font for body text.
3. Avoid all eccentric, smart-alec fonts.
4. Use print that's big enough to read.
5. Have about 10-14 words per line.
6. Use line spacing of about 1.2 multiple lines.
7. Use headings in bold with space above.
8. Limit the use of underlining, italics and block capitals.
9. Set text flush left and ragged right.
10. Use black print on white paper.
11. Balance the page as a whole.

Use plenty of white space

Be generous with white space. It really helps the reader—and it's free! If space is limited, better to eliminate some text than to sacrifice your precious white space—always!

Use wide margins on both sides, and top and bottom.

Break up pages full of type. When people see pages crammed full of grey type, they often skip those pages. They look boring. They look serious. They look like hard work.

You can break up large chunks of type in your document by using:

- subheadings
- shorter paragraphs
- indented quotes
- bullet points
- graphics.

Use a standard serif font for body text

Use a common serif font like Times New Roman or Palatino for body type, because these fonts are easy to read in paper documents—that's a well-proven fact. Use sans-serif like Helvetica or Arial or Verdana for contrast in specific places.

Serif fonts have little hats and shoes, which lead the eye forwards. The hats and shoes provide extra clues as your eye scans the text. Standard serif fonts suitable for body text include:

Times	Times New Roman
New York	Palatino

Use sans serif fonts for contrast

Sans serif fonts do not have little hats or shoes, and so they have a modern look.

Sans serif fonts are useful for contrast in headings, margin notes, tables, footnotes, and any other place where a very large or very small font is needed. Standard sans serif fonts include:

Geneva	Helvetica
Arial	Verdana

Use screen-friendly fonts for online documents

Certain fonts have been especially designed to be clearly readable on-screen, regardless of whether they are serif or sans serif.

These screen-friendly fonts are useful for writing e-mail, intranet pages and Web pages:

Geneva	New York	Mishawaka
Verdana	Georgia	

Also, for the sake of your eyes, you may want to work in one of these fonts when writing any large document, switching later to the paper-friendly font of your template.

Set your Web browser to display in one of the screen-friendly fonts—you'll immediately notice that text is easier to read. But don't make the mistake of printing letters, reports and other paper documents in Verdana, Mishawaka or Geneva, just because they're easier to read on-screen.

Use print that's big enough to read

People avoid reading fine print: they associate it with difficult and boring legal material. In general, use 10 point type or larger. If you're writing for seniors, use at least 12 point type.

Have about 10-14 words per line

About 10-14 words (or 50-70 characters) per line is perfect. There's a limit to the number of words that readers can comfortably follow in a line of type. If the lines are too long, readers tend to lose the thread. But if the lines are too short, many phrases are broken, and reading is disrupted.

In everyday business documents aim to use a single column of text that is between 120 and 150 mm wide.

Use line spacing of about 1.2 multiple lines

Space between lines helps readers to stay on the line. With single spacing readers may accidentally read the same line twice, or skip a line. Too much space and they get lost in space.

The ideal line spacing is roughly 1.2 lines, but it varies according to the font you use. In Microsoft Word, choose Format: Paragraph: Line spacing: Multiple—and type in 1.2.

Or you can add 10% spacing. In Word, choose Line spacing: Exactly: 13 pt with a 12 pt font, 11 pt with a 10 pt font and so on.

Use headings in bold with space above

Good design includes clear, consistent signposts. For headings to stand out, they must contrast with the body text. Using a larger font in bold generally does the trick. And you can use a different font. The reader intuitively knows which headings are the most important (the big black ones) and which headings are less important (the smaller, lighter ones).

Learn how to use 'Styles' in Microsoft Word. Word provides a hierarchy of styles for headings, making it very easy to be consistent.

Avoid the use of underlining, italics and block capitals

Use italics very rarely—for example, just for book titles or side quotes. Italics slow down reading. On a screen they are often completely illegible.

USE CAPITAL LETTERS WITH GREAT DISCRETION, IF AT ALL. AGAIN, THEY'RE HARD TO READ. THEY'RE OK FOR HEADINGS, BUT NOTHING ELSE.

<u>The only items you should ever underline in a modern document are hyperlinks on a Web page or intranet</u>. If you underline anything else, people will assume it's a hyperlink. Underlining for emphasis is an ugly hangover from the days of the typewriter, when there was no such thing as bold or a

choice of fonts. Underlining cuts through the downstrokes of g, j, p, q and y, making text hard to read.

If you want the effect of underlining a heading without the disadvantages, try using borders in Microsoft Word. The bottom border is set below the downstrokes of g, j, p, q and y. Example:

Set text flush left, ragged right

Print your letters, memos, reports and proposals so that:

- the left hand side of your document is a straight vertical line
- the right hand side of your text is uneven.

In other words, just like the text in this book. This format is highly readable, because the shapes of the words are standard, and the spaces between the words are even. Every individual word looks just the way it did when you learned to read.

Justified text is printed in a block with straight margins on each side. It puts a strain on readers, because the words and spaces have to stretch or shrink to fit the line.

Don't use fully justified text except in books or other published material—for example in magazines or annual reports or legislation. In any other context this format makes an aggressively formal impression.

Some people personally prefer full justification because it is 'tidy', and therefore they resist this advice. But the advice is based on neurological facts, and is not just a personal opinion. Know that if you justify the text of an A4 document, you will automatically alienate your readers and make them feel uneasy.

How about centred text? That can be useful for headings or items in a box, but use with caution because centred text is also difficult to read.

Use black print on white paper

Boring? Boring is best, because boring is easy to read. Good design does not intrude—you don't even notice it. Black on white is by far the best option for your main text.

Be cautious about using type on a shaded background. Even a pale grey shading decreases legibility. It can work with headings or highlighted quotes—but don't overdo it.

When using coloured text on coloured background, it must be high contrast: a strong dark colour on a light one. Certain colour mixes are unreadable by colour-blind people, and that includes at least five per cent of white males.

One of the least legible colour schemes is reversed print: white or coloured type on a black background. Frequently, readers simply skip words in this format.

Balance the page as a whole

Consider the appearance of every page as a whole. A page of text alone looks boring and timid. A page with long, solid paragraphs looks impenetrable. A page with too many bold headings is confusing, as if the writer can't decide what is the most important information. Too many bullet points on a page can fragment the meaning.

Don't go overboard with fancy formatting tricks. Use as few lines and boxes as possible. Practice restraint with tinted backgrounds, reverse type, tables and graphics.

The ugly letter transformed

On the next page you'll see the 'ugly' letter that appeared early in this chapter. It has lost that mean, pinched, hostile appearance. Now it looks readable—and that's the point.

Note that nothing fancy has been done. The format is highly conventional. Plain is beautiful, provided you follow the guidelines. The moment you try to do something fancy, things start to go wrong. (If you want something fancy, ask a professional designer.)

Berhampore Rehabilitation Center
22 Edinburgh Terrace Wellington
* * * * * * * * * * * * * * *

2 December 1999

Mr John Halitiris
Top Training Team
PO Box 9999
Bulls

Dear Mr Halitiris

Would you please send me any brochures or information relating to programmes your company is offering this year? I am particularly interested in training that increases employment opportunities.

Yours sincerely

B. A. Slough

B.A. Slough
Social Worker

8

Oral communication

Discussions with clients or customers

For all oral communication in a business setting, prepare if you possibly can. Ask questions. Listen to the answers. Use short sentences. Take notes. And pay attention to your body language.

Before an informal meeting with clients, gather any material you must give them. Note in advance:

- the information you must convey
- the questions you must ask.

Watch for body language signs that your message has got through—or not. Notice signs of discomfort or puzzlement or anxiety such as a frown, a glazed look, or loss of concentration. Check it out:

> Do you see what I mean?
> Would you like to hear more about ...?
> Are you comfortable with that?
> Do you have any questions about...?
> Have I explained that clearly enough?

Be absolutely certain you understand what the client is trying to convey. Paraphrasing the client's words is an excellent way to check whether you have got the message right. It's specially useful when there's conflict:

> So you're saying that...
> So you're concerned that...
> Let me check that I understand you correctly...
> Do you mean that...?

Body language also sends a message. The way you sit or stand can convey that you are alert and positive. (Or not.) If you find yourself mirroring the physical position of your client, don't fight it. This means you are empathising, which improves communication.

Informal meetings

No doubt you spend a great deal of time in informal meetings with colleagues. You know the time-wasters, distracters, stonewallers, bullies and burblers. By focusing on the process as well as the content of discussions, you can minimise frustration and speed up decision making.

Generally, somebody is in charge of team meetings. But in a team that's functioning well, everyone quite naturally takes some responsibility. You can do all the following without anyone even noticing:

1.	Clarify the meeting's purpose.	This meeting is to...
2.	Set limits.	Let's not discuss the budget today.
3.	Take notes.	
4.	Ask quiet people for opinions.	(Just an interested glance does the trick.)
5.	Curb those who talk too much.	Thanks, Charlotte.
6.	Ask people to clarify their comments.	Do you mean...?
7.	Keep the group on task.	Could we talk about that later?
8.	Watch the clock.	We've got five more minutes.
9.	Draw attention to relevant issues.	There's a risk that...
10.	Query the meaning of silences.	What are we thinking here?
11.	Seek consensus.	Do we agree that...?
12.	Summarise.	So we've decided...
13.	Outline the actions required.	So we need to...
14.	Allocate or claim tasks.	Who will...? I will...
15.	Boost morale.	Good thinking.

Using the phone

Focus totally on the voice in your ear—really be there for your caller! This can shorten the conversation. Take notes. Finish by summing up the call and restating what you've agreed on.

Believe it or not, body language is important even for phone conversations. People can hear the smile in your voice. Stand up and you'll sound more alert, more active.

Clarity is crucial. Your caller may be partly deaf, or may not understand English very well. You can train yourself to speak more clearly by speaking slowly and relaxing your jaw. Don't let your voice tail off at the end of a sentence—if people can hear the final word, they can usually hear the rest. (That's an actor's trick.)

Listen to your own voice on the phone, and if possible, tape it. Ask yourself whether this is the tone of someone helpful and capable.

As for your answerphone message, make it as brief as possible without being downright rude. (Long messages drive some people to phone rage, especially when it's one of a series of recorded messages.)

Formal meetings

'A committee is a group that keeps minutes and loses hours.' Milton Berle

In the course of your career you'll probably have to attend many formal meetings. Anyone—including you—can be nominated the minutes secretary. As well as knowing how to write agenda and minutes, you should know the basics of formal meeting procedure.

Principles of parliamentary procedure (in brief)

The purpose of parliamentary procedure is to make it easier for people to work together effectively and to help groups accomplish their purposes. Rules of procedure should help a meeting, not hinder it.

All meetings must be characterised by fairness and good faith. Every topic presented for decision should be discussed fully.

All members have equal rights, privileges and obligations. All members have the right to speak on any issue and to oppose any issue. The chairperson must give everyone at a meeting an equal chance to speak.

A majority vote decides most issues—but the rights of the minority must be protected. Sometimes members will ask the minutes secretary to note their abstention from voting, or their negative vote.

Before a meeting can conduct business it requires a quorum, i.e. a minimum number of members present.

A meeting can deal with only one matter at a time. Business is accomplished by means of debating motions. The word 'motion' refers to a formal proposal, moved by one member and seconded by another, that the meeting take a certain action. Normally, members may speak only once on the same motion, except that the mover can also be the final speaker.

Writing agenda

The agenda consists of the items of business to be discussed by a meeting. The chairperson is usually responsible for preparing the agenda. The usual form of an agenda is shown below.

AGENDA ITEMS	WHAT HAPPENS WITH EACH ITEM
Welcome	*Chairperson opens meeting and welcomes all.*
Apologies	*Minutes secretary notes those present and in attendance, and apologies.*
Minutes of last meeting	*Chairperson asks members to approve (or amend) the minutes of the last meeting.*
Matters arising	*Discussion of stand-alone matters arising from the minutes (excluding matters covered elsewhere in the agenda).*
Reports	*Financial report is presented first, then others. Copies are circulated, and a copy kept permanently attached to the agenda.*
Correspondence	*List of letters received and sent is circulated and discussed.*
Other items of business	*Other specific items are named in the agenda and discussed.*
General business	*This is the place to raise items that are not on the agenda.*
Next meeting	*Chairperson confirms date, time and place of next meeting.*
	Minutes secretary notes when the meeting closes or adjourns.

Writing minutes

Minutes in a standardised format must be taken of all committee meetings, annual general meetings (AGMs) and extraordinary general meetings (EGMs). Minutes of all meetings must be kept safe for future reference.

As the permanent record of an organisation's business, minutes are important documents with both historical and legal implications. They preserve institutional memory. They remind people of tasks and deadlines. They inform absentees about what happened at the meeting. They are studied by auditors.

As a legally valid document, the minutes must record the following:

1. Date, time and place of meeting.

2. Names of members present (i.e. those required to attend—for example, board members) plus those 'in attendance' (i.e. staff members).

3. Names of those sending apologies for absence.

4. Adoption of the previous meeting's minutes, and any amendments.

5. Summary of reports; the financial report must include actual expenditure and commitments to expenditure.

6. All elections and appointments.

7. Resolutions, motions and amendments: record these word for word, noting the mover and seconder in each case.

8. Votes for and against and abstentions, if required. Otherwise record decisions as 'It was agreed...' or 'The committee agreed...'

9. Items of general business raised.

10. Next meeting: date, time and location.

11. Time of closure or adjournment.

12. Name of person taking the minutes.

Summarising the discussion is not a legal requirement, but a common convention.

Who's responsible for the minutes?

The chairperson must sign off the minutes—but does not actually write them. The CEO (or registrar or secretary) is responsible for getting all the details right. In some cases a regular minutes secretary takes the minutes at every meeting; in other cases the job is rotated among members.

As minutes secretary, you write a first draft of the minutes, and give it to the CEO (or registrar or secretary). Very likely some changes will be made. Then the minutes are passed to the chairperson, who checks or amends them and signs off.

Minutes are a minefield of committee politics. Some people have a vested interest in being quoted a certain way, or being quoted frequently. They may try to influence you and subvert the process.

As minutes secretary, don't get embroiled in arguments. When Mr X phones in a rage, just say, 'Thank you for your comments. I'll pass them on to the CEO (or registrar or secretary).' Fortunately, it's not your problem.

Good minute taking requires high-level verbal, analytical and political skills. You are responsible for:

- including all the essential details
- summarising discussions accurately and concisely
- preserving the reputation of your organisation and your boss
- satisfying all members that the minutes are accurate and impartial—and sometimes, that's the problem!

Make your task easier by preparing for the meeting in advance. Read the minutes of the last meeting. Check how much detail the CEO requires, and whether you should write in the passive. Study the agenda.

At the meeting

During a formal meeting the job of the minutes secretary is to write, not talk. Write notes on the agenda and on blank paper.

You can't write the minutes if you don't understand what people have agreed. Don't hold back—ask for confirmation or clarification on the spot.

Whenever anyone moves a motion, ask for a copy if possible. Otherwise, write it down and check the wording at the time. Note the mover and seconder also. If a vote is split, record the numbers.

Note key points and all decisions, deadlines and agreements.

As a back-up, you can record the whole meeting on an audiotape. Pray that, having taken all necessary notes, you won't need to play it back.

And do all this without disrupting the flow of the meeting! (It's a big ask.)

After the meeting

Convert your notes into minutes. Use the company template, or the minutes template in Chapter 11.

List items in exactly the same the order as the agenda, using subheadings that correspond to agenda items.

Distinguish fact from opinion. Opinions are personal views. Attribute opinions to their source:

RIGHT Jane suggested that...
WRONG The group concluded that...

Use indirect speech. You don't need to record every word said (except for formal motions). Don't quote the exact words used in a discussion.

RIGHT Jane advocated appointing an HR manager immediately.
WRONG Jane said, 'We must appoint an HR manager immediately.'

Sometimes you are required to write minutes in the passive voice. This means you don't record who said what. Instead, you write, 'It was noted that...' or something similar.

How much detail should the minutes include? This varies greatly, and depends on the organisation's policy. Some want only the decisions recorded, not the reason for the decision (in other words, the legal minimum). Other organisations want full coverage of the discussion.

As a general rule, include enough information so that the minutes make sense to people who were not at the meeting. This often means writing a short sentence about the background before you record the decision made.

Approving the minutes of the last meeting

The CEO (or registrar or secretary) should duplicate the minutes of the last meeting, and circulate them to members before the meeting.

At the next meeting, the chairperson asks, 'Are the minutes of the previous meeting a correct record?' If no one objects, the chairperson states: 'There being no errors or omissions, I declare the minutes of the (date) meeting approved as printed.' If there is a mistake in the minutes, any member may point it out. The secretary then makes an appropriate correction or addition. The record will then read: '...approved as amended.'

Some organisations require a formal motion to approve the minutes. Somebody moves, 'That the minutes of the (date) meeting be approved as printed (or circulated).'

Making speeches and presentations

Does the thought of making a speech or a presentation terrify you? If so, the best help you'll ever get is from a public speaking club such as Toastmasters or Tecorians. You can actually have fun while overcoming your fear of public failure. In-house training can also be a great help.

Remember that a group of people is just a group of individuals. In your speech, address people in the audience individually, one by one. That's not so hard!

Preparation, as always, is essential. Check the room, facilities, time and numbers expected. Have a low-tech back-up plan.

Writing your speech

Write your speech first as notes or a mindmap. Make three main points, and allow yourself up to three illustrations or amplifications of each point.

You can't beat the old adage for a successful speech:

1. tell them what you're going to tell them
2. then tell them
3. then tell them what you told them.

You have heard this advice a thousand times. But it's surprisingly hard to put into practice, because by the time you actually give the speech, you have heard it so many times. It sounds familiar... too familiar. Remind yourself that your audience is hearing this speech for the first time.

Repeat the same key phrases throughout the speech. Use them like headings. Use repetition as a rhetorical flourish and a memory aid. In a speech, it's not a crime to repeat yourself—it's more of a crime to state your main points only once. After all, when reading a paper document, people can flick back to see what was written on an earlier page. But when listening to a speech, they rely on you to remind them what you said earlier.

To illustrate your points, use plenty of case histories, examples and stories. People are simple creatures. We remember anecdotes. We can deduce a generalisation from an anecdote, but not vice versa. We forget facts and numbers and generalisations if there's no story attached. So tell us a story!

You might want to write the whole speech out word for word, and rehearse from that. Deliver your speech to a tape recorder or mirror. Time yourself.

When you know the speech inside out, revert to your outline of key phrases written on cards, or a mindmap. Don't be tempted to read your speech—that is deadly for the audience.

Finally, you're prepared! You'll be great! Just enjoy the situation and learn from it. And as far as possible, be yourself. You are your own greatest asset. You're unique. You're interesting. You know your stuff. You're worth listening to.

Academic conferences

At academic conferences, people often expect you to read your paper, so that they hear exactly what they will read later. If you believe this approach is absolutely necessary, rehearse assiduously so that you virtually know your paper off by heart. Then you can deliver it with intelligence and passion.

Highlight key phrases, especially at the start of paragraphs. Just glance down at the next highlighted words, and look at the audience while you deliver that sentence. Do allow yourself at least the occasional paraphrase or short aside; this helps to humanise the occasion for both you and your audience.

And pause often, especially if you are tempted to read from the full, written speech in front of you. When you read a speech, you inevitably speak far too quickly.

Adapt your body language for international presentations

Be aware of your audience's expectations. In a different cultural context, or when speaking to an international group from mixed backgrounds, your natural body language may be quite inappropriate.

Most Western cultures value direct, personal eye contact and rather expansive, dramatic physical gestures. Many non-Western cultures find such behaviour uncouth or even offensive.

When addressing a Western audience, train yourself to meet the eyes of one person after another in the audience, until almost everyone feels you have personally engaged with them.

But if you are a Westerner and your audience is not, take your cue from the behaviour of the chairperson and other speakers. If your audience considers eye contact to be immodest or aggressive, you can still include everyone by sweeping your eyes gently over the entire audience. In general, be somewhat more formal in every way.

Westerners also need to adapt when making presentations in other English-speaking countries. What US citizens consider a direct, upfront and friendly manner can seem brash, insensitive and self-serving to a British audience. And a person with good old British courtesy may appear stuffy, aloof, cold, unassertive, insecure or wimpish to a US audience.

Be prepared for anything! Luckily, just four tips will carry you safely through most international presentations:

- prepare
- observe
- adapt to cultural differences
- and despite everything, be yourself. (It's you they want to hear, not some puppet or clone!)

Electronic presentations

Rehearse, rehearse, rehearse. Check all your equipment in the room in advance. Get there with tons of time up your sleeve. Never admit to feeling insecure with a datashow projector or computer. No need to boast—just assume it's easy and the hardware will function correctly. (And it will, if you've arrived ahead of time and checked every detail.)

Have you noticed how people hide behind their electronic slides? If you use a data projector, make sure it's only one part of your presentation. People want to see your face, and you need to see their faces too.

The presentation depends heavily on the quality of your slides. These had better be very good in every way. Whether you're using PowerPoint, Persuasion or some other programme, prepare a master slide that goes well beyond the basic Wizards. Make the slides attractive, consistent and readable.

Better not use full sentences on slides, or people will concentrate on deciphering the sentences instead of listening. Use phrases instead. (Four per slide is plenty.) Headlines should be no more than seven words long. Minor points should be no more than five words. And graphics are great, provided they clearly demonstrate a major point.

In general, follow the rules for modern page design in Chapter 7. But here are some special guidelines for slides:

1. The most legible fonts are sans serif, bold, with some variation in stroke thickness.

2. Light text on dark ground is OK, but be sure there's a strong contrast.

3. Don't overuse colour. Just use it to emphasise. Use colours that complement your logo.

4. Never use solid caps or italics or a script font. (What's the point of a great set of slides that nobody can read?)

5. Left align text.

Team presentations

Frequently you're not making a presentation as an individual, but as part of a team. The team approach is in some ways easier on everyone involved, but it requires just as much preparation, if not more.

As your team begins the process of preparing for a presentation, you might want to look back at the guidelines for being a useful member of a discussion group. (You'll find them early in this chapter.) Together, you'll need to sort out the following points:

1. Who's your audience, and what's special about them?

2. What do they need, and what do they want to hear?

3. What are the three main points you need to convey?

4. Summarise your message in one pithy statement (try for twelve words or fewer).

5. Who will lead the team?

6. Who in the team is best qualified to speak on which issue? Who wants to speak on which issue?

7. What form will this presentation take? Other than in words, how can you convey the level of commitment to the client's problem? What's your theme, and can you demonstrate this dramatically, graphically and professionally? Do you need the inspiration and assistance of a PR person or graphic artist?

8. Who will be responsible for all the practical and technological details of this presentation? Who will make sure the room is ready and the audience will turn up and the refreshments are ready and the datashow actually works?

Consider the template for sales presentation slides in Chapter 11. Perhaps you will never follow exactly this pattern, but it's an excellent starting point. If you use this template for your presentation slides, and you have a presentation team of three members, you might allocate responsibilities as follows:

Introduction, plus slides 1-3: Team member #1 (leader)
Establish rapport with audience; introduce team members; outline what each person will talk about; demonstrate your understanding of the client's business and requirements; prepare the audience for your solution.

Slides 4-7: Team member #2
Summarise in one or two sentences what Team member #1 said; present your solution; focus on three aspects most significant to your client; analyse the benefits to this particular client.

Slides 8-11: Team member #3
Summarise in one or two sentences the points made by the preceding speaker; explain all the financial aspects of the solution; stress value for money and give an appropriate cost analysis; outline the strengths of your company and why your company is ideally placed to assist the client.

Slides 12-13, plus closure: Team member #1 (leader)
Summarise efficiently and persuasively every main point made by the preceding speakers; emphasise the specific benefits of specific services to this specific audience; explain the next step which the audience needs to take in order to gain these benefits; thank the audience for its attention; invite the audience to ask questions or discuss the presentation.

In a team presentation there's no room for ad libs or digressions: you cannot make unilateral decisions on the wing. If you're tempted to answer a question at great length half way through your speech, you must consider how that affects other team members as well as on the impact of your group's presentation as a whole.

With a team, you can assume that your rehearsals will be extremely fruitful. Give each other feedback on whatever factors you decide are important. Remember that everyone contributes in different ways: personal styles may differ considerably and still be effective.

In rehearsal, team members can evaluate and help one another with:

- professionalism: confidence with material and technology
- empathy: appreciation of this audience's needs and expectations
- voice: audibility, pitch, speed, authority, pleasantness
- personal manner: posture, grooming, eye contact, mannerisms
- content of speech and slides: accuracy, clarity, consistency, tone
- timing: get it right!

Leadership is important. The audience usually feels safer when one person is clearly the leader. The leader isn't the boss, but controls the timing and group dynamics, and both starts and finishes the presentation.

Interviewer and interviewee

An interview is a two-way thing. Whether you're the subject or the object of an interview, the same tips apply:

- prepare thoroughly
- visualise success
- rehearse
- dress appropriately
- attend to body language.

If you're interviewing candidates, analyse their CVs and check their references. If you're job-hunting, study the company. The more you know about them, the more they'll like you. Have your questions ready. As interviewee, don't hold back. It's fine to ask about salary and training and promotion prospects and job conditions—but do include broader questions that show you've researched the company's services and policies.

Visualise success. Positive visualisation is a tried and true method used by successful business people, and it's standard practice in professional sport. Visualisation is easy and it's free. It takes only a few seconds at a time. Banish all negative expectations, and picture yourself at the interview, confident and relaxed. Saying all the right things. Making a great impression.

For an important interview, have a real rehearsal with a friend. Practise answering curly questions. Stop and think before you reply—that proves you're not a parrot.

We are all swayed by what we see. It's only human. Give yourself maximum credibility through your appearance, choosing fairly conventional clothes. Strong handshake, eye contact, posture. They all suggest the type of person you are—alert, positive, strong and upright. (Of course.)

International interviews

If your interview is with someone from a different country, exactly the same body language may signal arrogance and insensitivity. Check it out! Question your colleagues, research through the Internet, read books, get some training—do whatever you can to prepare for the interview.

Fortunately, this works both ways. Both of you are trying to adapt your behaviour to the other culture.

So there's no need to go overboard in your attempt to behave appropriately—sometimes, trying too hard can be counter-productive. Just be sincere, be sensitive, be yourself. If you're obviously making an effort, this will surely be appreciated.

9

Getting it right

At last we get to grammar

Grammar appears late in this book because if you follow the guidelines for plain English, you're much less likely to make grammatical errors.

The word 'GRAMMAR' has a great capacity to frighten people. Many otherwise sensible people worry far too much about their grammar.

As a rule, you're likely to make grammar mistakes for just three reasons:

1. you wrote a sentence that was too long
2. you have a few bad habits
3. you have vague memories of 'rules' that are now out of date, or wrong, or optional.

Most grammar errors in business and academic writing occur in long sentences. So here's the best tip of all: keep all your sentences under 21 words. It's comparatively easy to control the grammar of a short sentence.

Who cares if you can't tell a gerundive from a geranium? This knowledge doesn't improve your writing one jot. Think more about writing clearly, and less about grammar. You can usually dodge the danger zones by rephrasing.

Above all, be aware that grammar is not a religion or a fixed set of moral rules. It's merely a guide to current conventions. So you need to know just enough grammar to:

- make a good impression
- avoid annoying people who do understand the niceties of grammar
- convey your message clearly, without ambiguity.

Ten serious grammar mistakes

Not many, are there? But these errors are very common, and they get noticed. You must get these right or your writing will seem sloppy.

1. Stop runaway sentences

Run-on sentences are two sentences end to end, often with a comma in between. But commas don't join sentences! To join two sentences you must have a word such as 'and', 'but', 'or', 'yet' or 'because'.

RIGHT	We have received your order. We will despatch the plants this afternoon.
RIGHT	We have received your order, and we will despatch the plants this afternoon.
WRONG	We have received your order, we will despatch the plants this afternoon.

To find where you need a period or a comma, read your own writing aloud, exaggerating the pauses. Ask a colleague for help, if necessary.

2. 'However' needs a cap and a comma

Another serious error is using an adverb to join two sentences. Adverbs don't join sentences! 'However' is the commonest culprit.

RIGHT	June was mostly fine. However, July was rainy.
WRONG	June was mostly fine, however, July was rainy.

EASY FIX

Always put 'However,' at the beginning of a new sentence and follow it with a comma. Then you're sure to get it right. (If you put 'however' in mid-sentence, there's a high chance of making a grammar mistake.)

3. Get itsy bitsy 'its' correct

How do you know when 'its' needs an apostrophe? You must get this one right, and you can!

EASY FIX

'Its' and 'it's' belong to two different families. One family has apostrophes:

He's, She's, It's.

The other family has no apostrophes:

His, Her, Its.

To check whether you need an apostrophe, run through the family tree.

He's fine. She's fine. It's fine. (Apostrophe required.)

His hat. Her hat. Its hat. (No apostrophe required.)

ANOTHER EASY FIX

'It's' (with apostrophe) is always short for 'it is' or 'it has'. Always. The apostrophe replaces the missing letters.

It's your turn. It's been too long.

4. Put apostrophes in their place

It's important to get all apostrophes right, for clarity as well as correctness. You want to write 'the employees' obligations' or 'the CEO's diary' or 'the children's curriculum'. Where does the apostrophe go?

EASY FIX

To find the right spot for the apostrophe, reverse the phrase like this:

The obligations of the [..................]

An apostrophe (or an apostrophe+s) goes after the exact word or phrase in the brackets.

the obligations of the [employee]	the [employee]'s obligations
the obligations of the [employees]	the [employees]' obligations[15]
the diary of the [CEO]	the [CEO]'s diary
the playground of the [children]	the [children]'s playground.

More about apostrophes later in Punctuation.

5. Trap the wandering 'only'

If 'only' wanders into the wrong position, confusion often follows. Theoretically, the whole meaning of a sentence changes if you accidentally put 'only' in the wrong spot.

Only the new manual confused the PA. (The old one didn't confuse her.)
The new manual only confused the PA. (It didn't spoil her day.)
The new manual confused only the PA. (It didn't confuse other staff.)
The new manual confused the only PA. (There was only one PA.)

Each sentence above is grammatically correct and each has a different meaning. The problem is, people can take the wrong meaning very easily.

When speaking, your emphasis and tone of voice shows exactly what you mean by 'only'—regardless of word order. Therefore in conversation, it doesn't matter if 'only' is in the 'wrong' position. Indeed, the correct version often sounds klunky when you say it aloud.

[15] Why not add another 's' to employees'? Because that would sound crazy. Trust your ear.

However, when the same sentence is written, suddenly the position of 'only' can change the whole meaning. There is no tone of voice on the page. But readers often imagine a certain tone of voice in their mind, and that can override the grammatical meaning of the sentence.

You get no brownie points for being grammatically correct if people persist in misunderstanding. If you have the slightest doubt, use the easy fix.

EASY FIX

Nine times out of ten you can simply remove the word 'only'. The meaning will still be clear and you save time.

> The new manual confused the PA.

Other wandering adverbs can also be troublesome, e.g. 'just', 'still' and 'even'. Again, the simplest solution is to remove the word from the sentence.

6. Me me me, not I myself

Psychological factors make this an extremely common error.

WRONG Please send a list of staff addresses to Paul and I.
RIGHT Please send a list of staff addresses to Paul and me.

EASY FIX

To check which is correct, remove the other person or people in the equation. The right answer will then be obvious:

> Please send a list of staff addresses to [REMOVE 'Paul and'] me.

Many people try to avoid the issue by writing 'myself' or 'yourself'. That's equally bad, if not worse. It's grammatically wrong, and (oops!) can be interpreted as a sign of a poor education.

WRONG I'll send a list of staff addresses to Paul and yourself.
RIGHT I'll send a list of staff addresses to you and Paul.

'Myself' and 'yourself' are correct in only two situations:

1. To emphasise or contrast: 'Paul knows everyone, but I myself am new here.' 'Your sister has blue eyes, but you yourself have brown eyes.'

2. When you're doing something to yourself: 'I ask myself...' 'You set high standards for yourself.'

7. Items on a list must be a matching set

This is another 'must'. A non-parallel list can be ambiguous and vaguely disturbing—besides being grammatically incorrect.

A list always has either a heading or a stem. The stem is the start of a list, and every item on the list must finish the sentence perfectly. (This is true regardless of whether you use bullets.)

WRONG The Ministry of Grammar approved verbs, nouns, and punished those who misused them.

RIGHT The Ministry of Grammar approved verbs and nouns, and punished those who misused them.

As you see, even a short, simple list can go wrong—and trouble is almost inevitable when you write a long or complex list.

WRONG The Ministry of Grammar ordered a customised style guide, 50 dictionaries of phrasal verbs, and arranged for consultation with the Journalists' Training Organisation.

EASY FIX

Write the sentence with bullet points (just as a test) and then make sure the first words of all the bullet points 'rhyme'. In this example, the words 'ordered', 'ordered' and 'arranged' are parallel, or rhyme.

WRONG The Ministry of Grammar:

- ordered a customised style guide
- 50 dictionaries of phrasal verbs
- arranged for consultation with the Journalists' Training Organisation.

To achieve parallel construction, this list needs an extra word to start the second bullet item:

- ordered 50 dictionaries...

The need for parallel construction applies even in sentences with only two items. Accidents happen when the writer is striving for a literary effect or when the main thought is interrupted by extra phrases.

WRONG You can choose between increasing the heat or, on the other hand, to reduce the quantity.

RIGHT You can choose between increasing the heat and reducing the quantity.

RIGHT You can either increase the heat or reduce the quantity.

8. Each and every one is singular

This common problem requires some tricky footwork. When we use words like 'each', 'every', 'everybody', 'nobody' or 'anybody', we're thinking about a number of people or things. But all those words are grammatically singular: they refer to just one person or thing at a time. And unfortunately, if you change the verb to correct the grammar, you create a pedantic phrase like 'he or she' or 'his or her'.

EASY FIX

Don't struggle over the grammar. Instead, make your point some other way.

WRONG	Everyone must clean their shoes.[16]
RIGHT BUT FUSSY	Everyone must clean his or her shoes.
EASY FIX	All guests must clean their shoes.
EASY FIX	You must clean your shoes.

WRONG	Each invoice must have 'PAID' stamped over their number.
RIGHT	Each invoice must have 'PAID' stamped over its number.
EASY FIX	Each invoice must have 'PAID' stamped over the number.
EASY FIX	All invoices must have 'PAID' stamped over the number.

'Neither' and 'either' present a similar problem.

WRONG	Neither of my shirts were clean.
RIGHT BUT TRICKY	Neither of my shirts was clean.
EASY FIX	Both my shirts were dirty.
EASY FIX	I didn't have a clean shirt.

9. Get tricky subjects to agree with their verbs

Certain annoying words are usually singular but sometimes plural.

RIGHT	The committee has approved expenditure of $11,000. (Singular, because all the people on the committee acted as one.)
RIGHT	The committee have gone on holiday. (This usage is unusual. 'Committee' is plural here, because the people acted as separate individuals.)

Some subjects seem plural but in certain kinds of sentences are really singular. Trust your instinct. Write what you'd say when talking.

RIGHT	Ten dollars is plenty.
RIGHT	Two litres is a lot to drink.

Sometimes the subject of a sentence has two parts: a singular phrase and a plural phrase. Again, write exactly what you would say. Provided English is your first language, your instinct will usually be correct. You'll naturally

[16] This usage is common and increasingly accepted. It is favoured as a way of avoiding sexist language. However, it is technically wrong and may annoy your readers.

match the verb to the phrase immediately before it—in which case the grammar will be correct.

RIGHT	Neither the topsoil nor the plants have arrived.
RIGHT	Neither the plants nor the topsoil has arrived.

Make sure your starter phrase refers to the very next word

Often you'll want to start a sentence with a starter phrase followed by a comma. If so, the phrase MUST refer to the word (or phrase) that comes immediately after the comma. (Be specially wary when your introductory phrase includes a word ending in ' -ing' or '-ed'.)

If you get this wrong, you can accidentally write a very silly sentence. This error[17] causes more red faces than miscommunication. Still, not a good look.

WRONG	Sprinkled with chopped coriander, kids love these potatoes.
RIGHT	Sprinkled with chopped coriander, these potatoes are popular with kids.
WRONG	As a putative social historian, this was just up my alley.
RIGHT	As a putative social historian, I liked this style of research.

And that's all?

Yes, that's all! When you have conquered these ten common errors, your chances of making a grammar mistake drop dramatically.

Some minor grammar points

'Which' or 'that' or 'who'?

When do you write 'which' and when do you write 'that'? Just bear in mind that too many 'whiches' can sound pompous, and too many 'thats' can sound choppy.

Don't worry about the rule. True, there is a rule, but it's broken more often than it's followed. Even the distinguished editors of Oxford University Press often ignore or perpetuate 'which/that' mistakes, so why should you care about getting it right?

Here's an example from Michio Kaku:[18]

---

[17] Known as a misrelated or dangling modifier.

[18] *Visions: How science will revolutionise the 21st century and beyond.* ISBN 0-19-288018-7.

WRONG	To more fully appreciate the importance of these developments, it is necessary to distinguish between MIT's robots, which are true *automatons* which can act independently, and the industrial robots on Detroit's automobile assembly lines, which are preprogrammed.

The above sentence has three 'whiches'—in itself a stylistic misdemeanour that the editor should have noticed. (I admire Michio Kaku so I'm blaming the editor.) The second 'which' should have been a 'that'. But any one of the easy fixes below would have improved this sentence.

EASY FIXES

When it's important to be correct, use any one of these tips.

- Always put a comma before 'which'.
- Never put a comma before 'that'.
- If 'that' or 'which' sound equally right to you, choose 'that.'
- If in doubt, shorten the sentence or chop it in two.
- Or rephrase to avoid using either 'that' or 'which'.

WRONG	I missed the deadline which ruined my reputation.
RIGHT	I missed the deadline, which ruined my reputation.
WRONG	I missed the drugs, that ruined my reputation.
RIGHT	I missed the drugs that ruined my reputation.

When do you use 'who'? When referring to people, of course.

RIGHT	The man who fixed my car.
OK	The man that fixed my car.
WRONG	The man which fixed my car.

Whom

As for 'whom', it's virtually obsolete. Authorities tend to agree that you might as well stop trying to use 'whom'. At best you'll sound pretentious. At worst you'll make a grammar mistake.

Punctuation

What a difference punctuation makes! Take this now-famous sentence:

a woman without her man is nothing

According to legend, women punctuate it the first way, and men the second way:

A woman! Without her, man is nothing.

A woman without her man is nothing.

This section contains a few guidelines for punctuation in business writing. If a particular punctuation mark causes very few problems, it won't be mentioned here.

The general trend today is towards fewer punctuation marks. Modern computer design conveys much information that was previously conveyed by apostrophes, commas, periods and semicolons.

Apostrophes in titles

Apostrophes are disappearing from names, titles and logos. (Maybe it's because an apostrophe can look very odd in a logo.) Ignore the grammar rules: just copy from the company stationery or phone book listing.

For example, Zino's restaurant has an apostrophe but Wakefields restaurant does not. Christchurch Girls' High School has an apostrophe, but Wellington Boys & Girls Institute Inc. doesn't.

Apostrophes in time phrases

Should you write 'two weeks' work' or 'two weeks work'? It's now OK to drop the apostrophe as long as it doesn't look funny.

A grammar buff can justify this radical step by saying that 'two weeks' can be regarded as an adjectival phrase, not a possessive phrase. We're not talking about 'the work of two weeks', but about 'two-weeks-sort-of-work'.

RIGHT	one week's work
WRONG	one weeks work[19]
RIGHT	two weeks' work
ALSO RIGHT	two weeks work

Apostrophes are not needed in abbreviations

When you're adding an 's' to an abbreviated title, an acronym or a date, there's no need to add an apostrophe. There's no grammatical reason or visual reason to insert an apostrophe. In fact, the apostrophe looks silly.

The following words are perfect the way they are. They are clear and correct.

RIGHT PCs, 1990s, QCs, CEOs, LANs.

The only snag is that your word processor hates you adding an 's' to a two letter acronym. It changes 'PCs' to 'Pcs' as fast as you type it.

[19] Why is this wrong? Because it looks peculiar.

EASY FIX

For abbreviations that you frequently pluralise, keep typing and apply 'change all' when you've finished the document.

Alternatively, just continue typing the next word. Then go back and retype that second letter (the capital C in PC). Provided you don't retype the space directly after it, 'PCs' will stick.

EASY FIX

Use the same trick when you want to start a word with an apostrophe. Examples: 'em, 'air-raising.

First type 'th'em' or 'h'air-raising'—then just delete the initial letter(s). The apostrophe stays the right way around.

Bullet points

What a joy is the bullet point! But what about punctuation? Bullets appeared after most standard grammar books were written, so people punctuate them in every possible way, even within a single document.

Actually, bullets remove the need for extra punctuation marks—because bullet points themselves are punctuation marks. But some writers use all the old punctuation marks PLUS bullet points. That can look very fancy, fussy and confused.

TOO FANCY

Bullet points are:-

- Useful;
- Easy; and
- Clear.

For bullet points that are phrases, not complete sentences, I prefer the following version, which is both common and correct. The colon and full stop are not strictly necessary, but they satisfy some primitive craving for closure.

RIGHT

Bullet points are:

- useful
- easy
- clear.

However, it's OK to leave out the colon, or the final full stop, or both. Just be consistent within the document! The worst thing you can do is punctuate every bullet point list a different way. Don't try to cover all bases: make a decision, and stick to it.

When the bullet items are complete sentences, the lean, clean punctuation system above won't work. In such cases, the following punctuation is simple and functional. A colon isn't necessary because it is obvious that the bulleted items depend on the sentence immediately before.

RIGHT Bullet points are easily abused for the following reasons.

- When items on the list are not parallel, the reader gets confused.
- When bullets are overused, bullet fatigue sets in and readers are inclined to skip to the next piece of prose.

It's not always easy, punctuating bullet points. To achieve consistency within your organisation, include examples in the company style guide.[20]

If you're having difficulty, perhaps you're using bullets inappropriately. Bullets are ideal for a short list of short points following a stem. But bullets are pointless when your points are paragraphs, and each one takes up half a page.

Don't spatter bullets as if from an AK47. If you have more than six consecutive bullets, you'll shoot yourself in the foot. People will forget how your list began, and the whole purpose of using bullets is defeated.

Do use the bullet tool in your word processor—hyphens look amateurish. And never use a double layer of bullets within bullets. The impact is lost.

You can't use the bullet tool in e-mail. Using asterisks is a good solution.

Bullets or numbers?

Use bullets where you want to make a few points of roughly equal importance. A numbered list implies that items are in order of importance, or in chronological order. Use numbers for procedures, showing what to do first, second, third etc.

Capital letters in titles

When do you write 'Minister', 'Secretary' or 'President' with an initial capital, and when do you write the same words without a capital?

First port of call is your corporate style guide. It should contain simple rules for capitalising any titles you are using frequently. Your style guide takes precedence over all other rules.[21]

---

[20] See Chapter 10.

The Ultra-Conservative Approach is to Capitalise Everything That Twitches, for example, all titles within your own organisation: 'Deputy Secretary of the Hinds Philosophers Association Supper Committee'.

Capitalising departments and sections of your own organisation is common: 'Department of Non-Restrictive Phrases and Clauses'. However, even government departments are modifying this old policy nowadays.

Print journalism (in newspapers, magazines and so forth) generally takes an extremely modern approach to capitalisation, and many organisations follow the same style. It's deliciously simple.

- At first mention, write the full name of an organisation, with capitals, 'Ministry of Grammar' or 'Hinds District Court'.
- Thereafter use either an abbreviation without capitals ('the ministry' or 'the court') or the initials of the organisation ('MOG').
- Don't capitalise titles: 'secretary', 'president', 'chief warden'.
- Don't capitalise sub-sections within an organisation: 'the department of gerunds and gerundives'.

Modern corporate practice tends to follow the conservative model when referring to in-house titles and departments, and the journalism model when referring to external organisations.

Colons

Colons (:) are becoming comparatively rare in business writing, except at the start of a list of bullet points. Elsewhere, modern formatting options make the colon an endangered species. Do we care? Not particularly.

Commas for clarity

Don't get hung up over obscure comma rules that you vaguely remember from way back. This is the golden rule of commas: use a comma to make your meaning clear or to prevent ambiguity. This simple, sensible rule overrides all others.

There's no point using a comma (even if an ancient grammar book says you should) when your prose would be perfectly clear without it. If you're not sure whether your sentence needs a comma, leave it out.

---

[21] See Chapter 10.

It's worth remembering that a comma often clarifies meaning in the following situations.

1. After an introductory word or phrase.

RIGHT	By a lucky coincidence, ...
RIGHT	However, ...

2. Separating an incidental, 'by-the-way' comment from the rest of the sentence. If the comment is in mid-sentence, you must have two commas (or two brackets or two dashes). However, it's usually a bad idea to stick extra information into the middle of a sentence, so don't overuse this sentence pattern in business English.

RIGHT	Mr Kim, our colleague from Hanoi, will be in the office next week.

3. Before 'which' or 'who'. (But not before 'that'!)

RIGHT We chose the Alambra dining suite, which is most uncomfortable.

4. To separate items in a list.

RIGHT	They brought their sheets, pillowcases and old pyjamas.
ALSO RIGHT	They brought their sheets, pillowcases, and old pyjamas.

Dashes

The occasional dash in a comparatively informal business document can be rather dashing. But don't—overuse—the dash—or you'll seem—scatty, or—mystical—like the poet Emily Dickinson.

Should you put a space before and after the dash — like this? Better not, because your word processor may decide you meant a hyphen, and change it accordingly. The true dash is designed to look handsome without those spaces. It's called an em-dash, and is as wide as the letter 'm'.

Please use a proper em-dash, not a hyphen. The em-dash looks more professional. On a Mac, press option+shift+hyphen. On a PC, press Control+Alt+the number pad minus sign. Or on any computer with Word, you can select Insert: Symbol from the toolbar, and click the em-dash.

It's no use trying to use an em-dash in e-mails or documents in Notepad or SimpleText. Instead, use two hyphens between two spaces -- like so. In html, the em-dash can be also be a little tricky. The double hyphen is, again, an easy alternative.

Periods (full stops)

Love them. Use them often. Use one at the end of every sentence. The period will get you out of many a pickle.

But do start removing the period from abbreviations such as PhD, MD, St, Mr, US, UK, pm, am, TV. This is the modern way.

RIGHT At 6.30 am[22], Mr Joe Alzheimer, PhD entered the headquarters of the Ministry of Grammar (MOG) and booted up his PC.

Is there any confusion here, with periods deleted? I think not. Retain the period only when readers might otherwise be confused.

After a period, type one space. Not two. The two-space habit is a hangover from the days of the typewriter. On a computer, spacing is precisely calibrated and one space looks just right.

Most lower case abbreviations usually retain their periods—perhaps because they look like little words, and therefore can confuse the eye. For example, most authorities still recommend periods in 'i.e.' and 'e.g.' I suspect a shift to 'ie' and 'eg' is inevitable sometime soon.

Numbers

There are four traditional rules for writing numbers. Sometimes two rules are mutually exclusive, so you are forced to break one of them.

RULE #1

Write numbers 0 to 9 in roman letters: one, two, three... The probable reason for this rule is that 1 and 0 can be mistaken for letters.

WRONG My choices were reduced to 1.

RIGHT My choices were reduced to one.

This rule has many, many exceptions. You read them every day. For example, in various contexts, all the following are correct:

RIGHT	Section 1	p1	page 1	Chapter 1
	$2	2 cents	2c	$2 million
	3 per cent	3%	3:1	.3
	4.00 am	4am	4 July	4 ft 7 in
	Grade 5	5-1 (in sport)	Series 3	Super 7

[22] The following are also fine: 6.30am, 6:30am, 6.30AM, 6.30AM, 6.30AM, etc. The important thing is to be consistent.

Except for 0 and 1, digits stand out clearly in a page of prose, which is useful when you're scanning a document with your eyes. For this reason, some organisations choose to have their cake and eat it too:

The select committee received two (2) submissions.

RULE #2

Write numbers in Roman letters (a, b, c, d, e...) when they occur at the beginning of a sentence:

RIGHT	Fifty infinitives were split.
WRONG	50 infinitives were split.

This rule is important: don't break it. In practice this means rephrasing some sentences, so that you simply do not start a sentence with a number. The rule probably arose because a period can be confused with a decimal point.

WRONG	Marian's dress cost $30. 20 people complimented her on it.
RIGHT	Marian's dress cost $30. Twenty people complimented her on it.
EASY FIX	Marian's dress cost $30. She received 20 compliments about it.
EASY FIX	Marian's dress cost $30, and 20 people complimented her on it.

RULE #3

Write numbers from 10 up as digits: 10, 11, 12, 13... You don't need to break this rule very often, thank goodness.

RULE #4

Be consistent when writing numbers that occur quite close together. When in doubt, favour digits, because they are more obvious in the text.

WRONG	between the ages of eight and 99
RIGHT	between the ages of 8 and 99
RIGHT BUT FUSSY	between the ages of eight and ninety-nine
WRONG	chapters six-23
RIGHT	chapters 6-23

Quotation marks

'Single quotation marks' or "double"? Different grammar and usage books give contradictory rules. You can't even legitimately claim there's a British way as opposed to a North American way.

So take the easy way out. Use single quotation marks. The benefits are:

- they look modern
- you don't have to press 'shift'
- you can change all quotation marks and apostrophes to curly quotes with one action.

Then the only time you'll ever need double quotation marks is for HTML or for a quote within a quote. The latter rarely occurs in business writing, but for the record, here's an example:

RIGHT 'What is a "technicolour yawn"?' she asked.

Ignore any other rules you have heard about using single or double quotation marks. They are finicky, they're hard to remember, they're rarely applied and they don't make sense. Trust me—the above rule covers everything. In a rare case where you hit a problem, don't rush to the grammar book. Instead, just rephrase the sentence to avoid the problem.

Semicolon

You can live a rich and satisfying life without ever using a semicolon, unless you are an academic. However, the semicolon still has one useful function. In certain formal documents—for example, legal documents—the use of bullets may be forbidden. Luckily, a semicolon can differentiate among items in a complex list.

RIGHT The plaintiff claimed that her ex-partner had removed from her office 32 pencils and 32 whiteboard markers; 4 boxes each of A4 manilla envelopes and regular white window envelopes; and a cubic metre of polystyrene packing chips stored in a clear plastic bag.

Editing and proofreading

Editing and proofreading are on a continuum that blurs in the middle. Whether you are acting as editor or contracting an editor, be very clear about the brief. What do you mean by 'editing' for a particular job? A considerable amount of time and money may be at stake here.

At one extreme is a big editing job that may entail checking and correcting facts, restructuring the document, removing redundant sections and even adding new content. At the other extreme is proofreading. Technically, proofreading is reading the final proofs of a document just before printing, when you expect only a few typos will need changing.

Actually, when most people say 'editing' they often mean minor tinkering—about Stage 3 as explained below. All the more reason for clarifying the brief before you start. Just how far is the editor expected and permitted to go?

Here's a horribly common scenario: the writer of a report sincerely believes that it's almost perfect, and contracts a wordsmith to proofread it. Now the wordsmith discovers that sections of the report are arranged in an illogical order, some information is inaccurate, headings are misleading and a large chunk of the document is superfluous. Will the budget cover the necessary changes? Will the writer's feelings be hurt? As a wordsmith, always check and double-check your brief, and insist on assessing any job before you commit to doing it.

As the writer of any big document, assume that you will always need expert help from a wordsmith, and earlier rather than later.

When you try to edit your own writing, you are in double jeopardy, because you 'know' what you wrote—that is, you know what you think you wrote. You may be literally incapable of reading the actual words on the page.

With an important document, demand some editorial assistance. At the very least, ask a colleague to read your draft and highlight anything that is confusing. Ask someone to consider the questions raised in Stage 1 below. A colleague's instinctive response could save your bacon.

When editing, print out your document and work from hard copy. Don't try to edit or proofread from the screen—that's hopeless. This is a fine-muscle task, and reading is much more difficult on the screen. What's more, you can't get a grip of a whole (large) document from a screen.

A major editing job happens in stages. You can't possibly examine every aspect of a document at once.

Editing: Stage 1

Stage 1 is sometimes called 'macro-editing'. It's your first step with any editing job. Study the big picture—always from the reader's point of view. Analyse the entire document, and see how the sections or parts relate to the whole. Consider the total impact of the document.

1. What is the purpose of this document? Does it achieve its purpose?

2. Would some major change help this document to achieve its purpose?

3. What is the most important message in this document? Is it obvious? Is it emphasised? Or is it buried?

4. Does the document have an appealing, appropriate, and highly readable appearance? Is the formatting excellent, or does it require some major change? Would colour, graphics or illustrations improve it ?

5. Is the structure ideal from the reader's point of view? Do any sections need repositioning? Does the document begin with a summary of the whole? If not, why not?

6. Does this document contain all the necessary information? If not, what's missing?

7. Is the information accurate? Is it logical and proven?

8. Are any sections unnecessary or irrelevant?

On the basis of your analysis, you may then take radical actions such as:

- restructuring the entire document or certain sections
- adding material
- removing material
- writing or rewriting the executive summary.

Editing: Stage 2

Next, focus on headings and paragraphs. Again, look at the more important and general factors first.

1. Are headings and sub-headings appropriate and powerful?

2. Are there enough sub-headings?

3. Does every paragraph make one main point? Are paragraphs well structured with the main point usually placed first?

4. Are paragraphs in the best order? Do paragraphs flow naturally?

5. Are there any unnecessary paragraphs? Are there any unnecessary sentences? (You bet there are!)

6. Are any paragraphs too long?

Then you can do the following jobs as necessary:

- rewrite headings so they are explanatory and powerful
- insert additional sub-headings
- delete delete delete paragraphs and sentences to your heart's content
- re-arrange the order of paragraphs and create smooth transitions
- restructure paragraphs.

Editing: Stage 3

Now you've dealt with the big things and the moderately big things, you can deal with matters of style and tone. Consider sentences and words—are they OK? If not, fix them now.

These are picky little editorial tasks, but rather satisfying. If the document was written by a committee, you now convert it from a camel into a race horse. You'll make the style consistent in such matters as passive verbs, contractions, and sentence length.

According to what you discover, you will do some or all of these:

- shorten or split over-long sentences
- delete delete delete superfluous phrases and words
- correct grammar mistakes
- reduce the number of passive verbs
- remove or change fancy, old-fashioned or ambiguous words
- rewrite negative sentences in the positive.

Follow your house style rules, or by default the rules of plain English.

Essentially, this completes the editing. Now you move on to proofreading.

Proofreading

Proofreading can be regarded as Stage 4 of the editing process. The proofreader assumes that all the big things in a document are correct. Again, proofreading is best done in stages. This is a very difficult and demanding task that requires strong concentration.

If you proofread often, it's well worth learning the main proofreading symbols: this speeds the task and makes your meaning absolutely clear.[23]

Your job is to impose consistency and correctness on:

- spelling
- punctuation
- format
- grammar (in case anything was missed in the editing stage).

First print out the document with generous line and margins. Mark the errors clearly on the page.

---

[23] In any standard editor's style book (e.g. *Style Book,* Wallace and Hughes, ISBN 1-86956-123-6)

Proofread in perfect conditions. Remember that proofreading is extremely demanding, highly unnatural work. In real life your goal is to read quickly—but when proofreading, you have to forcibly slow down. In real life you read for meaning—but when proofreading, you ignore meaning and focus on such petty things as commas and font size.

In a perfect world you would do the following. Go to another room. The board room. An interview room. Somewhere away from the phones. Clear the desk, except for:

- a highlighter, sharp pencil, rubber, ruler and sticky memo pad
- your house style guide
- a modern dictionary
- the proofreading checklists in this book
- blank paper for your style sheet.

Here two useful ways to slow down your reading and concentrate on detail.

1. Cover the page with a sheet of paper, revealing one line at a time.
2. Read the text aloud, slowly, just two or three words at a time.

Use a style sheet

Essential when proofreading, the style sheet is the simplest possible device. Are you supposed to write 'gaol' or 'jail'? '4.30pm' or '4.30 PM'? Whenever you notice a recurring error or inconsistency make a note of the correct version on your style sheet. This enables you to standardise spelling and punctuation. Use an old-fashioned sheet of paper marked up like this:

<table>
<tr><th colspan="3">SAMPLE STYLE SHEET</th></tr>
<tr><td>ABCD
capitalize
cooperate
(the) CEO</td><td>EFGH
focused
gaol
Figure 1</td><td>IJKLM
inquire
long-term (before noun)
long term (anywhere else)</td></tr>
<tr><td>NOP
online
PCs</td><td>QRST
toolbar</td><td>UVWXYZ
word processor</td></tr>
<tr><td>NUMBERS
1990s
US$5 million
11 am
12-year-old
9 per cent</td><td colspan="2">NAMES, ABBREVIATIONS, IMPORTANT TERMS
MOG =Ministry of Grammar
QMS =quality management systems
Ms Ariadne Simpson, QC
CYPFAS</td></tr>
</table>

How long does proofreading, editing or writing take?

This depends on the document and the level of intervention required. Most editors have a fixed hourly rate, and will quote for a job after they have studied the document. Skilled wordsmiths usually charge more per hour, because they do the job faster. And when you find a fine wordsmith, treat with care and generosity! They are not exactly thick on the ground.

Be sure to allow sufficient time, whether you do the job yourself or engage someone else to do it.

proofreading	Correcting all errors: a last-minute check before printing	about 17 minutes per 1000 words to proofread twice
copy editing	Correcting spelling, punctuation and small grammatical errors in professionally written documents.	about 35-60 minutes per 1000 words
editing	All the above, plus rewriting ambiguous sentences, and restructuring some sentences, paragraphs and sections.	about 1-2.5 hours per 1000 words
major editing	Restructuring in a logical sequence, rewriting, checking content against external references, adding information that was omitted.	about 2.5-4 hours per 1000 words
Optimising Web content for search engines	Writing html titles, meta tags, alt-text, and link-text. Researching, selecting and prioritising keywords. Editing body copy for keywords.	about 30 minutes per page, regardless of length
Web content editing	Editing or rewriting content for the Web, from documents provided by the client. Editing for skim-reading, credibility, plain English, and tone.	about 1-3 hours per page
Web content writing	Writing Web page content from scratch on behalf of the client or in consultation. Selecting source material, and writing and editing Web page content.	about 6-12 hours per 1000 words

Tips for writing faster

By reading this far, you've already learned many crucial tips that will help you to write more rapidly. If you've started following the guidelines in *Crash Course in Corporate Communications*, you'll probably find you are now working faster. Basically, you've stopped wasting time.

But a word of warning!

Maybe your company or organisation has been using an old-fashioned, clichéd, jargon-filled style of writing for many years. And some people can write quite fast if they never think about what they actually mean.

It does take a little time to undo bad old habits and learn good new habits. As you start to take communication seriously, your writing may actually slow down for a time. Don't panic: this is only a temporary setback.

Keep yourself on track by adopting systems for writing. You can't remember everything at once, so use the templates and checklists in this book. Then watch your success rate rise and costs fall as your clients and customers find they can understand your documents at first reading!

To save time when writing, do things in their proper sequence.

Most people aim to get a document right at first attempt—bad idea! Ultimately you will save a great deal of time if you treat writing as a process with several stages. In brief:

- think very hard before you write anything
- plan the structure
- then blurt it out
- and finally edit what you have written.

To write fast, write in stages

1. Think first! What's this document's purpose, audience, and intended result? What's your brief? Thinking first stops you wasting time writing the 'wrong' sort of document. And if you think first, you won't write something too long.

2. When possible, use a template as the basis. Obviously you will sometimes need to depart from the template—but there's no need to reinvent the wheel.

3. Outline your document, using only phrases. Never write a sentence till you've got the structure of the document right. (If you cut and paste complete sentences, they always need changing later.)

4. When you're ready to write, write rapidly. Imagine giving someone the same information over the phone, and write just as you'd speak. DON'T waste time editing yet. If you can't think of a word, don't stop—push on. (Getting stuck is often a sign that you're repeating yourself.)

5. When you've finished scribbling, edit the document. Treat editing as a separate stage. You don't have to remember everything! Use the checklists, which cover all important points.

Save time with your word processor

A few hours' training in using your word processor software efficiently can save you heaps of time—days, weeks, months!—in the long run.

Why type every letter of the name of your organisation every time it occurs? Use macros or the auto-correct function on your word processor. For example, you can arrange that every time you type 'pmhc' it's converted instantly to 'Prime Minister Helen Clark.' And so on.

If you keep making the same mistake, or discover you've been inconsistent in spelling a certain word, use 'find and change all' in your word processor toolbar.

To keep your headings consistent, use the Styles function. Don't change every heading manually by bolding it and increasing the font size. Just apply 'Heading 1' or 'Heading 2' or 'Heading 3' (that's enough levels!) instead of the 'Normal' style. And don't worry if those headings have the wrong look. You can change them all at once when the document is finished.

Using Styles has many benefits. The word processor can instantly create a table of contents, complete with page numbers. And for large documents, the Outline view of documents shows all the headings at a glance. In Outline view, you can easily shift whole sections of your document around.

10

Corporate responsibilities

Corporate communications tasks

Crash Course on Corporate Communications deals mainly with content and some aspects of design. This chapter explains some of the broader responsibilities of the corporate communications staff.

The modern communications department of a large corporation or public sector organisation is a remarkable organism. Combined, staff members have a great range of skills—in IT, editing, writing, marketing, design, publishing, Web design, public relations and journalism. Staff with various mixes of these diverse skills must work closely together. All these skills are necessary to communicate successfully within the organisation, and with clients, the media and the general public.

Smaller organisations often outsource some of their communication responsibilities.

The corporate communications department is generally responsible for achieving excellence in:

- information management
- communication technology
- style and content of all communication, in-house and external
- design of corporate documents
- production and distribution of corporate documents
- storage and archiving of corporate documents.

Taking the broad view

Corporate communications decisions are closely linked to decisions about information management software and training. 'Documents' are not just letters and memos and reports on paper: the word is now used for all electronic data, whether for billing, accounting, stock, HR, plant, archives—the list is almost endless.

Electronic information management is largely beyond the scope of this book, but senior corporate communications staff certainly need to be knowledgeable in this field. So do all managers, consultants and professional people, and even people running a home business. At the very least, you need to know when you need help!

Look at it this way. If you're an accountant, for example, your entire business consists of gathering, managing, creating, using and communicating information.

Bear in mind the enormous cost of poor communication, and the widespread concern over online security and privacy. These points alone suggest that corporate communications involve a great deal more than meets the eye. Your business survival depends on acquiring the right communication skills, hardware and software—and keeping them all up to date and in top condition.

For example, how do you know when a document becomes obsolete? How can you be sure that outdated documents don't keep circulating? When should old documents be archived, and when should they be shredded? How do you know if a particular document is the latest version? You need to create a system for updating corporate documents. What's more, you need a system for monitoring the updating process. Then staff must be trained to use it.

Consider the following list. Although it is just a small sample of corporate communications responsibilities, it gives some clues to the range of tasks.

1. Develop communications policy and procedures that advance the corporate plan.

2. Identify and purchase (or commission) cost-effective software for creating documents and managing information, and train staff to use it.

3. Create new templates for memos, letters, reports and proposals. Search and destroy old templates on staff computers.

4. Create a style guide and distribute it to all staff through the Intranet.

5. Rewrite all standard letters and forms in plain English, and test with target users.

6. Train all new staff in plain English business writing.

7. Contract a six-monthly audit of corporate documents.

8. Contract an archivist to store corporate documents on CDs.

9. Develop and implement a policy on staff Internet use.

Developing communications policy and procedures

One corporate communications task is to develop a communications policy for the whole organisation. Clearly, for a large organisation this is a major task. Corporate communications departments need policies and procedures that go well beyond the urgent tasks that dominate daily life at the office.

The policy of corporate communications must always be closely related to the strategic direction of the organisation. First, be sure you clearly understand that direction. Next, analyse what the organisation requires you to do to further the corporate plan. Then you analyse the communications department's current procedures, note where they fail to match the corporate plan, and make plans accordingly.

Say management is committed to winning more clients. Communications officers analyse how their own current practice fits this commitment, and develop communications strategies that will help to fulfil management's goal of expansion. After those strategies are approved, the communications department is responsible for implementing them.

When you're ready to start developing or adjusting your communications policy, you may go through the following steps.

1. Scope the job.

2. Identify communication issues where current procedures hinder the corporate plan.

3. Develop procedures in response to each issue.

4. Decide who will be responsible for implementing each procedure.

5. Decide in what order the procedures will be implemented.

6. Establish milestones and deadlines.

7. Decide how to monitor your progress.

8. Then get cracking!

First, write about one page summing up the issues involved and the direction you will be taking. Secondly, create a detailed list of specific procedures, under three headings: Issues, Procedures and Responsibility. An example follows.

Issues	Procedures	Responsibility
Standard letters do not reflect the company's new image.	Rewrite all standard letters in plain English.	CC Chief Editor
Application form causes many inquiries, wasting staff time.	Engage professional wordsmith to rewrite application form in plain English and test it on valid sample of customers.	CC Chief Editor
	Print new application forms and distribute to all branches.	CC Publications Manager
	Ensure all old application forms are destroyed.	CC Archivist

Corporate style guide

Every organisation needs guidelines for style in corporate documents. Your goal is to achieve a consistent, appropriate style for all corporate documents. A good design guarantees that your documents have a certain recognisable 'look'. A corporate style guide (or house style guide) helps everyone to achieve an appropriate writing style and tone, one that typifies the organisation.

Crash Course in Corporate Communications covers the vast majority of issues of corporate style—but it doesn't always lay down the law. Instead, an acceptable range of options is suggested. Every organisation must make many decisions on house style.

The biggest headache for the corporate communications team is not producing a style guide, but ensuring that all staff use it. You need to develop foolproof procedures for keeping the style guide constantly up to date and constantly in the minds of all staff. Unless someone takes responsibility for this, the style guide gets lost and forgotten within six months. Make sure the style guide is in a user-friendly form, and is easily accessible online.

What is a corporate style guide?[24]

Typically an organisation draws up a short list of essential rules for staff, and circulates this both on the Intranet and in hard copy.

Even the shortest style guide should contain the following:

1. A model letter with correct format.
2. Guidelines for appropriate style (e.g. use of passive and 'you').
3. Information about templates.
4. The authorised form of commonly used titles, with rules for capital letters.
5. The authorised form of technical words, abbreviations and acronyms.
6. The authorised form of other frequently used words, dates, times etc.

The style guides of public sector organisations may contain detailed rules and conventions for writing official and parliamentary documents.

Team writing

Many large documents are created by a team. Reports, policy papers, proposals—often they're the work of many people. The corporate communications staff may be involved as part of that team, or take over after the writing is finished. The writing team needs to meet frequently to monitor progress and discuss issues.

[24] Also known as a house style guide or style manual.

Among their first tasks, team members will:

- clarify their brief
- outline the document
- decide who writes what
- set deadlines, milestones and limits
- make sure everyone uses the company style guide.

As writing proceeds, team members should:

- write quickly and simply
- compare style sheets and settle controversies
- offer work in progress for feedback
- give feedback to other writers especially on content and structure.

Towards the end, team members will re-evaluate these issues:

- Is the structure ideal?
- Have we put first things first and last things last?
- Is the content appropriate, accurate and complete?
- Have we included all that is necessary and no more?

Then the editing process begins. Give this important responsibility to one person: you cannot edit as a team. (Editing is a bit like conducting an orchestra.) Ask the best writer on the team, your precious PA, someone in your corporate communications section, or an outside wordsmith.

The editor must make the style consistent. At this stage, the document is a hotch-potch. Some team members write plain English like a dream. Others use the passive compulsively, or bury their key sentences in the middle of paragraphs, or have other annoying mannerisms.

The editor must also remove repetition. Several people may have made virtually the same point in different parts of the document. And that is why, when you're writing in a team, there is no point in agonising over your style. Very good is good enough until the editor moves in and starts cutting.

Train your writers and monitor the results

Chapter 1 gave examples of the huge savings possible when communication is improved. Conversely, poor communication may be costing your company hundreds of thousands of dollars per year.

Logically, then, training in business writing should get high priority. Everyone who writes regularly should receive some training. The corporate communications department usually takes some responsibility for training employees and managers in the skills of business writing. For many, this is their first encounter with plain English. 'Why didn't I learn this at school?' they cry.[25]

Busy executives benefit from a short, concentrated online course based on their own genuine documents, or a couple of hours of personal training.

Be sure to consolidate the results of training. Training in plain English writing brings a return in hard cash. To make sure of this, some structured supervision, monitoring or peer review is desirable. Otherwise the daily grind can defeat the trainee, and bad habits may return.

A regular documentation audit assesses the impact of training on the quality of your corporate documents. A wordsmith assesses a sample of documents against agreed criteria, and reports on how your organisation is doing. The audit is a realistic basis for planning training programmes.

Documentation and quality management

Documentation and quality management cannot be disentangled. They are closely intertwined at every level.

The ISO9001 Standard states its requirements for document control, and is a significant guide for quality management systems. The ISO9001 approach is useful even if your organisation is not contemplating accreditation.

Your documentation policy must include specific procedures to:

- plan documentation procedures
- write documents
- design documents
- update information
- distribute information (on paper and online)
- store information.

After deciding on procedures, you will develop detailed systems to monitor progress, and to make sure people meet their commitments and deadlines.

[25] My theory is that at school, most English teachers love literature. And so, no matter what the curriculum, they are subconsciously trying to create clones of Katherine Mansfield or Henry James. Plain English training is inclined to contradict everything a literary English teacher tries to teach. (It takes one to know one.)

11

Templates and examples

This chapter contains both templates and good examples of various types of documents.

Your company style guide must take precedence over these templates and examples: all documents must maintain the corporate identity. However, in many organisations the style guide:

- is non-existent or lost
- or is never consulted
- or needs modernising.

If any of the above situations applies in your organisation, someone (you?) had better initiate steps to create or update the style guide. And you can use this chapter as a starting point.

The templates guide you in three important ways:

- format and page design
- content: what MUST go in your document
- structure: the default order of items within your document.

The report and proposal templates follow the 'happy compromise' path. They are suitable for any organisation, no matter how conservative or how modern.

All the examples are good models of layout, structure and style. Use the examples and templates:

- to compare with your own documents
- as inspiration when you are stuck
- as a quick check when writing or formatting a document.

Template: standard business letter[26]

your printed logo and address may be at top, bottom, left, right or centre	CORPORATE COMMUNICATIONS PO Box 6559 • Wellington • New Zealand office@writing.co.nz http://www.writing.co.nz
date	9 March 1999 *two blank lines* *(no attention line)*
name	Stephen Arbanji
title	Training Officer
company	Ariolan Head Office
postal address	PO Box 80-990 Melbourne 6998
	two blank lines
formal hello line	Dear Stephen Arbanji
OR informal	OR Stephen *one blank line*
subject line/no 'Re'	**Training your staff in modern communication skills** *one blank line*
audit-trail sentence	Thanks for your letter inquiring about my training services.
	one blank line
key message	We provide in-house courses and executive training in modern corporate communications, successful international communication, and writing copy for the Web. *one blank line*
action	I would like to discuss your company's unique training requirements with you in person. Please e-mail me (office@writing.co.nz) so we can arrange a time to meet. Sometime between 10-14 September would suit me well. *one blank line*
extra information	*(Useful but not essential information goes here.)*
goodbye phrase	Sincerely OR Kind regards OR Yours sincerely *four blank lines*
signature	*Rachel McAlpine*
name	**Rachel McAlpine**
title	Director

[26] See Chapter 3. Feel free to adapt this template for your style guide.

Example: e-mail message[27]

> Marion
>
> Here is the information you requested yesterday.
>
> 1. The seminar on IT careers for mature people will be held on 30 July at GRUA headquarters, 22 Scots Terrace, Fairlie.
>
> 2. Special report 'Tax Breaks for Tea Breaks'. You can order this now from mailto:aolivio@grua.org.au. Cost: $40.50 including GST and postage.
>
> Regards
>
> Andreo Olivio
> Executive Secretary GRUA
> 22 Scots Terrace, Fairlie, South Canterbury
> www.grua.org.nz

Example: business letter conveying simple instructions

> Dear Katherine Mansfield
>
> **Authors' Fund: 1999 re-registration**
>
> Our records show that we have not yet received your re-registration for 1999. This matter requires your urgent attention.
>
> Please complete and return the enclosed form by 27 June 2001. Then your new books will be included in the 2001 library survey.
>
> Yours sincerely
>
> **Janne du Fresne**
> Administrator

[27] See Chapter 3.

Example: business letter conveying simple information[28]

Dear Mr Serepisos

Funds transferred to your bank account

We received your withdrawal request on 16 October 2002. We completed the following transaction the same day. Please keep this letter as confirmation of your transaction.

Funds withdrawn from Ship Toprate Account 16 October 2002
and transferred to your nominated bank account # 090909 09
on 16 October 2002 by electronic transfer

$12,606.30

The unit prices relating to this transaction are those applying on 16 October 2002, the date we received your withdrawal request.

[28] See Chapter 3.

Example: simple thank you letter[29]

Revella

Thank you so much for your generous donation of books to my school. Your generosity is really appreciated and the books will fit easily into our Library/Reading programme.

Although we live and work in an impoverished community, as teachers we still try to put quality material in front of our children. My staff and I believe that literacy is a key to beating the social disadvantages many of our pupils suffer from. To this end we budget between $10,000 and $12,000 annually for reading materials.

Donations such as yours enable us to provide even more!

I would like to meet you and thank you in person, if you're ever in the Porirua area.

Kind regards

Terry Von Trapp
Principal

[29] See Chapter 3.

Example: letter conveying complex ideas and information[30]

Xavier

How Mountcorp's debt recovery service can help you

Thank you for inquiring about our collection services. We have the nation-wide representation and telecommunications systems to trace your debtor, recover your debt and report back to you.

I have enclosed:

- a Collection Instruction form with terms and conditions on the reverse
- guidelines for completing the form
- a reply-paid envelope
- a brochure explaining our services.

We need from you:

- the Collection Instruction form, completed and signed
- copies of invoices or other documents that support your claim.

We charge 20% commission on the debts we recover, whether they are repaid to Mountcorp or you. We charge an additional $10 each on debts under $50. If you cancel your instructions to us, we normally charge a closure fee of 5% of the outstanding debt.

If we undertake legal action for you, we'll charge the costs to you and then attempt to recover them from the debtor on your behalf. In any event, we will seek your approval before incurring such costs or any other extra charges.

All you need to do is complete and sign the enclosed form, attach supporting documents, and return all items in the envelope provided.

Yours sincerely

Huia Pinelli

Manager, Debt Recovery Services

[30] See Chapter 3.

Example: memo conveying complex information[31]

FINANCIAL PLANNING UPDATE

Changes to Unit Trust Taxation

If you hold units in any New Zealand-based unit trust, note that the government made a change to taxation, effective 1 April 2002.

The change is substantially a technical one. Most clients will be affected very little. It will affect you if:

- you are (or could be) classified as a trader
- or if you are on a marginal tax rate of less than 33%.

No doubt you have received information on this from various fund managers. Of all the information produced, we think the booklet produced by Ontoit Investment Managers is the best—largely because it's brief and easy to read! If you'd like a copy, please advise us.

Electriflexi Bonds

Do you hold Electriflexi Bonds maturing 15 June 2005?

If so, and you're subject to resident withholding tax (RWT), we recommend that you sell or switch your holdings before they mature.

Why? When the bonds were originally issued, a portion of their face value was deemed to be income (and thus subject to RWT). However, the RWT deduction is made only when the bonds are paid out at maturity. So even if you claim the RWT as a tax credit, you can't do so until after the March 2006 tax year.

We can help you avoid this problem by selling the bonds on your behalf before 31 May 2005. Please contact us as soon as possible for further advice.

[31] See Chapter 3.

Example: short memo report[32]

To	Paula Kitching, safety supervisor
From	Brian Dupont
Date	29 November 1999
Subject	Unsecured electrical cables in B2

Incident

On 28 November 1999, intern Jules Macarthur tripped over a loose electrical cable in Room B2. He was taken to Accident and Emergency and found to have a cracked rib.

Findings

Inspection showed two electrical cords were lying unsecured on the floor. Room B2 needs at least two additional double power points to cope with new equipment. Other rooms in B Block have similar problems.

Action

I secured the loose cables in B2 with a plastic cover screwed to the floor.

Recommendation

I recommend that we install 4 new double power points in each room in B Block.

Priority: 1

Approved by (signature): *Paula Kitching*

[32] See Chapter 4.

Template: sections of a longer report

Remember, this is only a guide. Except for Sections 1, 2, 3 and 12, sections won't always be in the same order. Nor will sections always have the same names. See Chapter 4 and the template on the next page.

1. Title page	2. Table of Contents	3. Executive Summary
4. Introduction (brief, purpose, scope, background)	5. Background (optional)	6. Conclusions
7. Recommen-dations (optional)	8. Costs (optional)	9. Methods (optional)
10. Discussion	11. Conclusion (Optional)	12. Appendixes (if any)

Report template: title page[33]

interesting title that summarises the whole report	**Singapore schools are ready for Readit CD-Roms**
descriptive sub-title	*The right product and the right market for export opportunities online*
summary of what the report does	This report confirms the feasibility of selling Readit's educational CD-Roms through the Internet, and recommends an Internet marketing plan that targets Singapore schools.
name and address of client	*Report prepared for:* Readit Ltd PO Box 9999 Perthton 2001
name and address of writer	*Report prepared by:* Maria Caledonia Netlock Ltd PO Box 7765 Perthton 2071
date	22 December 1999
signature	*Maria Caledonia*

continued...

[33] See Chapter 4.

Report template: table of contents

Table of Contents

continued...

Report template, continued

section name	EXECUTIVE SUMMARY
heading: summarises findings	**Singapore schools are ready for Readit CD-Roms**
descriptive subheading	*The right product and market for export opportunities online*
summary of terms of reference and background	On 3 October 1999, Readit Ltd asked Netlock to examine the feasibility of selling Readit's educational products through the Internet, and suggest a marketing strategy. While ready to move online, Readit wants to avoid costly errors and maximise the value of its Web site.
summary of conclusions and recommendations	Netlock confirms that selling Readit's products through the Internet will be a profitable venture if well planned. We recommend developing a marketing plan that targets Singapore schools, and concentrates on selling educational CD-Roms.
summary of methods	Our recommendations are based on detailed analysis of rival products and potential markets, and supported by ten years experience in the field.
summary of costs	Estimated costs in the first 12 months include $25,000 for Web site and e-commerce development, plus about $170,000 in research and development. If a satisfactory arrangement is reached with Singapore's Ministry of Literacy, Readit can expect to profit from the investment within 18 months.
summary of discussion	Technological, cultural and financial risks must be foreseen and systematically minimised. Readit's CD-Roms will need some adaptation for global marketing, and a sound marketing infrastructure must be created. That said, Singapore schools and parents are a large, natural market for Readit's CD-Roms. They have the technology and the desire to boost educational standards in English. If Readit wishes to proceed with this venture, the next step is to develop a comprehensive Internet marketing plan.

continued...

in some reports, you may put this information in an introduction

TERMS OF REFERENCE

Required: a targeted, realistic online marketing strategy

On 3 October 1999, the Marketing Manager of Readit Ltd invited Netlock to:

- analyse whether e-commerce will be cost-effective for Readit
- identify Readit products suitable for selling online
- identify appropriate international markets for those products
- advise on developing an Internet marketing strategy.

in other reports, you may put this information in an introduction

section name

BACKGROUND

descriptive heading

Moving online—but where and how?

By October 1999, James Rowan, Readit's Marketing Manager, was aware that e-commerce was the way of the future, and that Readit's competitors were already trading online.

It was difficult to find accurate, up-to-date information about how successful e-commerce had proved in the field of educational goods and services. However, it seems that both the rewards and risks of selling online are potentially very high.

Readit wants to export appropriate goods to appropriate world markets, and does not want make any costly blunders. Readit requires a cost-effective Internet strategy that will expand its business and maximise the value of its Web presence.

continued...

section name	CONCLUSIONS
heading	**A timely, profitable, low-risk opportunity**
	Readit's chief competitor, Happyread Ltd, has been profitably selling books on the Internet for eighteen months. Readit could trade just as profitably, and with careful planning is likely to exceed Happyread's export sales turnover.
	Readit's CD-Roms are a popular product with a high profit margin and low handling costs. A major opportunity exists next year for mass sales to elementary schools in technologically advanced Singapore. We believe that Readit should seize this exceptional oppportunity before looking for any other markets. Singapore parents who want to improve the English of their pre-school and elementary school children could also be targeted.
	Success will depend on meticulous costing, expert technical support, skilled negotiation and culturally sensitive marketing. These are areas of potential risk.
section name	RECOMMENDATIONS
heading	**Target Singapore schools and promote CD-Roms**
	We recommend that Readit:
number recommendations either in chronological order (do 1. first, 2. second...) or in order of importance	1. Consult with the Singapore Teacher Resource Centre Director. 2. Prepare a proposal and presentation for the Singapore Minister of Literacy, to reach him by 16 May 2000. 3. Propose mass sales of the Romper Readit CD-Roms for state primary schools in Singapore, with full teacher training and technical support. 4. Consult with Singapore government officials over adaptation of Romper Readit CD-Roms. 5. Revise and repackage the Romper Readit CD-Roms expressly for the Singapore market. 6. Engage a Web site developer of long-standing, proven ability to design a Readit Web site with full e-commerce facilities.

continued...

Report template, continued

section name	METHODS
heading	**Experience, analysis and networking**
how information was gathered and analysed	Netlock has been involved in Web site development for ten years, and in e-commerce for about five years. We are leaders in the field, frequently consulted by the Minister of Communications.
may be any length, from very brief to the largest section	We consulted widely with experts nationally and internationally. (See Appendixes B and C.) We commissioned a market survey from the Department of Trade and Industry, and networked with educators and IT personnel in Singapore.
	We researched the Web sites of educational organisations worldwide, and studied the latest Annual Report and other documents of Happyread Ltd. The International Education Office of the Ministry of Foreign Affairs (NZ) provided valuable data and advice.
section name	ESTIMATE OF COSTS
heading	**Estimated costs in the first 12 months**
	Web site development $15,000.00
	E-commerce development $10,000.00
	Research and negotiations $70,000.00
	Product development $40,000.00
	Support services development $60,000.00
	TOTAL $195,000.00
	If a satisfactory arrangement is reached with Singapore's Ministry of Literacy, Readit can expect to profit from the investment within 18 months.
section name	DISCUSSION
heading	**Do it right or not at all**
	(Discuss all the issues here. This will often be the longest section.)
appendixes labelled A, B, C etc	*(Appendixes attached here.)*

Example: report title page[34]

Investment opportunities for superannuitants

Surcharge removal creates level playing field

This report analyses the impact of recent tax law changes and recommends four appropriate investment choices for mature people.

Report commissioned by:
Senior Investors Association
PO Box 98765
Auckland

George X. Jones, BCom, MBA
GXJ Accountants Ltd
PO Box 123
Hinds, South Canterbury

Signed________________________

Date: 1 April 2002

[34] See Chapter 4.

Example: letter report[35]

Dear Mrs Bartholomew

Property report: 19 Tarawere Street, Balmain

According to your instructions we inspected the above premises on Thursday 27 June 2002, including section, house and support. A summary of our findings follows.

Urgent maintenance required

Two items need your prompt attention:

1. Most of the electric wire is covered in fabric insulation. This is a fire risk. We urge you to engage an electrician to check all points and wiring, and find and replace all fabric-covered wiring.

2. Stains on the lounge ceiling suggest the roof has been leaking for some time. In the south-east corner of the roof, nails have worked loose, and we assume rain enters through these nail holes. Within 2-3 years the whole roof will need replacing. As a temporary measure you could have the roofing iron in the south-east corner patched, screwed to the roof bearers and silicone sealed.

Description and general condition of house and section

The house is a one-storey timber structure constructed in 1946. It is in good condition except for the roof and the electrical wiring. The roof is of galvanised iron corrugated steel sheet roofing. All flooring is timber on timber joists and bearers. External walls are timber framed and clad in timber weatherboards. Internal walls have been relined with gibraltar board. The house has recently been repiled. Plumbing was renewed in the 1970s and is sound. We saw no sign of borer or rot. The section is flat and well drained.

Yours sincerely

Bevan Wright
Consulting Engineer (Inspections)

Photos supplied:
A. *Nail holes and rust patches on south east corner of roof.*
B. *Stains on lounge ceiling.*
C. *Fabric-covered wiring.*

---

[35] See Chapter 4.

Template: proposals[36]

Be sure to create a great title page for every proposal or tender. This chapter includes a couple of title pages for reports: use those as a model.

Exciting title that summarises benefits to the client

Examples of titles

Increasing Network Reliability through Advanced Fax Capabilities

MWQ Sheetmetal—practical, cheap and trendy office fixtures

Finding the ideal sponsor for a chair in microbiology

EXECUTIVE SUMMARY

Interesting descriptive heading

Text

The executive summary summarises the entire proposal in 200-300 words. Write the executive summary last. It is the most important section. Make it lively, positive, interesting, accurate, complete, and crystal clear. This section should discuss items in the same order as they occur in the proposal.

THE ISSUES <CLIENT'S COMPANY> FACES

Brief, accurate heading summarising issues

Examples of headings

Anticipating the challenge of global competition

Meeting requirements for ISO9001

Can you afford to replace your ageing hardware?

Client expectations are changing every year

Text

State your understanding of what the client needs. State it right at the beginning and continue to state it all the way through. Rephrase the client's own words. List and discuss the issues or problems faced by this particular client, focusing on those that are relevant to your proposal. Use a descriptive subheading for each issue or problem.

continued...

[36] See chapter 5.

Template: proposals, continued

THE OUTCOMES YOU WANT

Heading summarising main outcome(s) wanted by the client

Examples of headings

Selecting the best hardware for the 21st century

Reducing accidents on the shop floor

Text

List and discuss the outcomes your client wants, as you understand them. Use a descriptive subheading for each outcome. State the outcomes in positive terms. State outcomes as headings in a long proposal or bulleted phrases in a short proposal.

Examples of subheadings

Maximum flexibility for graphics, text and financial data

Permanent, reliable, automatic archiving

PROPOSED SOLUTION

Heading summarising your solution

Examples of headings

Customised accounting software plus company-wide training

A complete and comprehensive PR package

Text

First, summarise your solution. Say how it solves the problem. Then, discuss the solution you propose. Use a descriptive subheading for each aspect.

BENEFITS OF OUR SOLUTION

Heading describing the benefits of your solution

Examples of headings

Direct and indirect savings guaranteed

Your production line streamlined and accidents reduced

Text

Describe all the benefits your client will gain from the solution you propose. Use a descriptive subheading for every benefit. Include facts.

continued...

YOUR INVESTMENT

Cost of our solution

Text

Spell out the costs in a brief and readable way. Tell the client exactly what your solution or product or service will cost, in money, time, people and other resources.

RETURN ON YOUR INVESTMENT

Value of our solution to <client's company>

Text

Show in a concrete way that the money will be well spent. Prove that your solution will improve your client's business results. Show as precisely as possible how much money your client will save, how much costs will be reduced, sales increased or profits boosted. Use graphs to make your point. Figures will impress here; slogans will not.

METHODS TO BE USED

Heading describing the methods you'll use

Examples of headings

National survey with detailed cost analysis

Refurbishment of all bedrooms and bathrooms

Text

Tell the client how you will implement the solution or provide the service. Show how your methods suit the client's requirements. Include milestones and resources. (This section may not always be necessary.)

ABOUT <OWN COMPANY>

Why choose <own company>?

Text

What makes your organisation different from your competitors? Be specific and consistent. Put reasons in order of their significance to your client.

Examples of headings

Unique value for <client company name>

Expertise and experience in...

continued...

SUCCESS STORIES

Interesting descriptive heading

Examples of headings

Psychometric testing raised Exford profits by 38%

Simplified insurance forms save Smith Ltd $578,000 per year

Our training reduced Picasso Hotel staff turnover 83% in six months

Text

Describe one or two case histories. Describe how you have helped a company with similar problems, and how the company has benefited. Use descriptive subheadings for each aspect of the story. Get permission from the client first.

SATISFIED CUSTOMERS

A list of <own company>'s references

Text

List three former clients as references, and invite your reader to contact them. Give name and address of each. Be sure to get their permission to list them as referees.

ABOUT <YOUR OWN COMPANY>

Interesting descriptive heading

Examples of headings

Creativity combined with commonsense

Reliability plus design flair

A mature firm with modern ideas

The undisputed leader in our field

Text

BRIEFLY describe your own company: its history, equipment, staff, experience. Mention only facts relevant to your client's situation. As elsewhere, use positive language. Double-check the so-what factor. Avoid lengthy corporate histories. (Nobody cares!)

Example: simple letter proposal[37]

Jane Ellice
Director
Webwow Ltd
2 Ailsa Ave
TUTURAMURI

Jane

Immediate Internet success is possible for Webwow Ltd

You advised me last week that Webwow is in the early stages of developing a raft of Web Design services. I understand that Webwow wants to gain credibility and enlarge its list of small business clients. While you are prepared to spend a year in the process, you want to see some benefits within six months.

My company can certainly help you to achieve this goal. We have the Web promotion know-how to complement your strong Web design skills and database management.

Our satisfied clients include TikTok Clock Candy. Within two years of implementing the e-commerce policy that we recommended, TikTok's annual export profits grew from $32,000 to over $200,000.

We can adapt your present Web pages for e-commerce. We will help you to create irresistible short-term special offers so that you quickly gain a portfolio of model Web sites and testimonials. We can focus your pages to attract small business clients. And we'll help you to turn your Web site into one of those information-rich, hype-free sites that people love to bookmark.

To achieve your goals you can expect to invest between $15,000.00-$20,000.00 over a period of 2 years. The return on your investment will come in the form of new markets, new clients, an international database and growing sales.

I look forward to meeting you next Thursday to discuss your project in detail.

Kind regards

Saul Latrobe
Consultant

[37] See Chapter 5.

Example: formal policy and procedures manual[38]

Norfolk Island Grammarian Registration Examinations

Information booklet
for overseas-qualified grammarians

Edition No. 3, December 1999

The Grammarian Council of Norfolk Island[39]
PO Box 97888
Norfolk Island

continued...

[38] See Chapter 6.

[39] Of course there is no such body. (Correct me if I'm wrong.)

Example: formal policy and procedures manual (continued)

Contents

continued...

Example: formal policy and procedures manual, continued

SECTION I

Grammarian Registration in Norfolk Island: legal background

1. This booklet describes the policy and procedures for the Norfolk Island Grammarian Registration Examination.

2. The Grammarian Council of Norfolk Island is the statutory body responsible for the registration of grammarians in Norfolk Island. The council examines each application on its merits as a separate case.

3. Section 200 of the Grammarian Act 1908 states that:
   'every person shall be entitled to be registered under this Act who satisfies the Council
   a) that he or she intends to reside and practise in Norfolk Island; and
   b) that he or she
      i. is the holder of a degree in grammar granted by a university elsewhere than in Norfolk Island; and
      ii. has, in the course of obtaining that degree, successfully completed a course of study that is equivalent to the course of study set down for admission to the Degree of Bachelor of Grammar of a public university of Norfolk Island; and
      iii. is registered in the grammarian register kept in the country in which the degree was granted, or there is good and sufficient reason why he or she is not so registered; and
      iv. has a reasonable command of the English language'

4. Under section 200(9) of the Grammarian Act 1908, the council must satisfy itself that:
   - you have sufficient knowledge and experience to practise in Norfolk Island
   - and you have a reasonable command of the English language.

5. If you graduated from any country except Australia, the USA or the United Kingdom, you will probably be asked to:
   - show your command of English by sitting an approved English test
   - and show sufficient knowledge and experience by passing one or more of the Norfolk Island Grammarian Registration Examinations.

continued...

Example: formal policy and procedures manual, continued

Three professional examinations

6. **English Examination (IELTS) or approved equivalent**
   This examination establishes whether you have a reasonable command of the English language (see paragraphs 19–29).

7. **NIG1 Written Examination**
   This examination establishes whether you understand the scientific basis of grammar.

8. **NIG2 Clinical Examination**
   This examination:
   - establishes how competent you are in using correct grammar
   - includes clinical, practical and oral examinations (see paragraphs 39–51).

Three types of Grammarian Registration

In Norfolk Island there are three types of grammarian registration.

I. Registration as a Grammarian
This type of registration enables you to practise as a grammarian in Norfolk Island without supervision.

II. Registration as a Specialist
After gaining registration as a grammarian, you can apply for registration as a specialist in a branch of grammar. You must satisfy the council that you have the appropriate qualifications, training and experience to justify registration as a specialist.

III. Temporary Registration
Temporary registration is described by clause 35 of the Grammarian Act, 1908. Temporary registration is limited to one year. In some circumstances, the council may extend temporary registration to a maximum of two years.

Temporary registration is normally granted only if you are coming to Norfolk Island:

- to undergo sponsored training for a specified period of time
- or to give instruction.

Example: instructions[40]

FIRE

If you discover fire:
Use the nearest fire alarm.

DIAL 111 and ask for fire services.

Leave the building.

Go to assembly area.

FIRE

If the fire alarm rings
Leave the building using the nearest Fire Exit.

Help disabled people to a safe place.

Follow wardens' instructions.

Use fire extinguisher or fire hose only if it's safe.

DO NOT use lifts.

DO NOT run.

ASSEMBLY AREA

- Willis Street
- on footpath
- in front of this building.

EARTHQUAKE

Move away from windows.

Shelter under a doorway or solid table.

Follow instructions of civil defence officers or floor wardens. Don't leave the building unless they tell you to.

(Fire alarms may go off in an earthquake.)

BOMB THREAT

Follow instructions of floor wardens, police officers or security staff.

If you get a phone threat, consult the emergency procedures manual near the phone.

If you find a suspicious object, consult the emergency procedures manual near the phone.

Study the emergency procedures manual BEFORE an emergency occurs.

[40] See Chapter 6.

Template: meeting agenda[41]

	AGENDA
who is meeting *what meeting*	Esoteric Society of Business Writers Annual General Meeting
place	at the Plain Language Foundation board room 1 Geodesic Street, Raratonga
time and date	**Tuesday 11 May 1999 from 3.30 pm to 5 pm**
agenda items must be in this order	1. Apologies
	2. Minutes of the 1998 AGM
	3. Matters arising
financial matters 1st	4. Financial report
other reports next	5. President's report
	6. Training Officer's report
	7. Election of Officers
prearranged business here	8. Regulation of verbs (*or whatever*)
	9. Applications for membership (*or whatever*)
other business (not prearranged)	10. General business
arranging the next meeting	11. Date and place of 2000 AGM
OR	*OR*
time and venue of next meeting (if already arranged)	Next year's AGM will be held on **Tuesday 9 May 2000** at the Plain Language Foundation board room, 1 Geodesic Street, Raratonga.

continued...

[41] See Chapter 8.

Template: minutes[42]

who is meeting	**Minutes** **Esoteric Society of Business Writers**
what meeting	Annual General Meeting
place of meeting	at the Plain Language Foundation board room 1 Geodesic Street, Raratonga
time and date	Tuesday 11 May 1999, at 3.30 pm
same order as agenda items *use 'Mr' etc. in formal minutes*	**Present** Dr Diane Lambie (Chair) Ms Akiko Kojimura Ms Audrey Kitchin (Treasurer) Mr Abel Eastcott Mr Jon Flesser
non-voting staff	**In attendance** Ms Sally Puhoi (Minutes Secretary)
apologies received from absentees	**1. Apologies** Miss Bonny Maloney
confirming the minutes is always the 2nd item	**2. Confirmation of previous minutes** The minutes of the 1998 AGM were approved as a true record.
minutes items often start with a brief background note	**3. Matters arising** The 1998 AGM had approved a reprint of the Society's grammar manual. Jon Flesser showed the new manual to the meeting, and confirmed the price of $22.95 to members and $43.95 to non members. Abel Eastcott volunteered to create a marketing plan. He will report to the Executive next month. ACTION: ABEL
always the first report; summarise it; all reports are later permanently attached to minutes	**4. Financial report** Audrey Kitchin presented the Society's financial report. Term deposits were receiving low interest, but sales of the manual would raise $500 in the current financial year.

continued...

[42] See Chapter 8.

Template: minutes, continued

summarise the main points made in the report	**5. President's report** Diane Lambie said the Society could take the credit for several significant plain English projects initiated by government. The Society would continue to act as advocate and training body for professional communicators.
typical two-sentence summary	**6. Training officer's report** This report showed that demand for training was up 30%, and another trainer was urgently required. Members agreed to contract a trainer to provide two training courses in June and August. ACTION: AKIKO
	7. Election of Officers The following officers were re-elected unopposed. Dr Diane Lambie (Chair) Ms Audrey Kitchin (Treasurer)
other items on the agenda	**8. Applications for membership** Jon pointed out that all new membership applications since 1980 had been refused. He proposed that membership rules be relaxed. It was agreed that membership be opened to anyone whose job involves communication in English. Jon will draft an amendment to the rules. ACTION: JON
miscellaneous items that are not on the agenda	**9. General business** Audrey suggested the Society should draft a module to teach understanding of the subjunctive. General opinion was that this was unnecessary.
	10. Date and place of 2000 AGM It was agreed that the next AGM would be held on 9 May 2000 at the Plain Language Foundation board room, 1 Geodesic Street, Raratonga, t 3.30 pm.
note the time the meeting ended	The meeting finished at 4.55 pm.

Template: sales presentation slides[43]

When giving your speech you will amplify most phrases with at least a sentence, or even a complete anecdote, example or explanation. Adapt the template to your own requirements, but respect the structure: it works!

Slide 1. Prepare to discover

(*This is where you tell them what you're going to tell them*.)

- how you can...
- how you can...
- how you can...

Slide 2. Your situation or problem

(*Why is the audience here?*)

- one issue faced by your client or audience (just a phrase)
- second issue faced by your client or audience (just a phrase)
- third issue faced by your client or audience (just a phrase)

Slide 3. You (or name of your client) need...

- the most important need of your client or audience (just a phrase)
- their next most important need (just a phrase)
- their next important need (just a phrase)

Slide 4. How we can meet your needs (or solve your problem)

- name your first product, service or feature
- name your second product, service or feature
- name your third product, service or feature

Slide 5. Benefits of <first product, service or feature>

- first benefit to client or audience (just a phrase)
- second benefit to client or audience (just a phrase)
- third benefit to client or audience (just a phrase)

Slide 6. Benefits of <second product, service or feature>

- first benefit to client or audience (just a phrase)
- second benefit to client or audience (just a phrase)
- third benefit to client or audience (just a phrase)

continued...

[43] See Chapter 8.

Template: sales presentation slides, continued

Slide 7. Benefits of <third product, service or feature>

- first benefit to client or audience (just a phrase)
- second benefit to client or audience (just a phrase)
- third benefit to client or audience (just a phrase)

Slide 8. Return on your investment

- first aspect of financial return (just a phrase)
- second aspect of financial return (just a phrase)
- third aspect of financial return (just a phrase)

Slide 9. Cost analysis

Graph: show an important aspect of client's return on investment

Slide 10. Cost analysis

Graph: show another important aspect of client's return on investment (e.g. a cost-benefit comparison between you and your competitors)

Slide 11. Our strengths

- your company's most significant strength, from your client's point of view (just a phrase)
- your next most significant strength (just a phrase)
- your next most significant strength (just a phrase)
- your next most significant strength (just a phrase)

Slide 12. Key benefits to you (or your customer's company)

(*Now you tell them what you've told them. Repeat phrases from earlier slides.*)

- most important benefit of your product, service, or idea (just a phrase)
- next most important benefit (just a phrase)
- next most important benefit (just a phrase)

Slide 13. How you can gain these benefits

(*State what your audience must do to buy the product/engage your services.*)

Put your business card in the hat/sign the form/pay now (whatever)

12

Checklists

'Common sense is genius dressed in its working clothes.'
Ralph Waldo Emerson

Most of these checklists are designed for use:

- after you've thought about the document you need to write
- after you've planned and outlined the document
- and after you've written your first draft.

But never mind that—use them any way that helps you!

With a checklist at your elbow, you are not alone.

Use the index to find the checklist you need now.

Checklist for writing plain English[44]

☐ 'you' and 'I' and 'we'

☐ 'you' more than 'I' and 'we'

☐ 'please' and 'thank you'

☐ common, simple, familiar words except for essential technical terms

☐ no wordy phrases

☐ very few abstract nouns, e.g. words ending in
-tion, -ment, -tion, -ance, -ence, -ance, ancy, -ency, -ity, -ism

☐ mostly active verbs (not passive)

☐ short sentences (21 words maximum for business documents)

☐ logically structured sentences (first things first)

☐ positive language

☐ concise language

☐ no unnecessary information

☐ contains all the information the reader requires

☐ content organised in a logical sequence

☐ inverted pyramid structure (usually)

☐ only one idea per paragraph

☐ plenty of explanatory headings

☐ lists and bullet points when appropriate

☐ readability: Grade 10-12 for general audience

☐ easy-to-read design

☐ correct grammar

☐ correct spelling

☐ correct punctuation

[44] See Chapter 2.

Checklist for writing business e-mails[45]

- ☐ new subject line (no Re: re: re...)
- ☐ subject line tells all
- ☐ short and concise message
- ☐ short paragraphs
- ☐ blank lines between paragraphs
- ☐ no solid caps except headings
- ☐ avoid adjectives and adverbs (they can arouse emotions)
- ☐ check content and tone before it's too late
- ☐ remember that 'deleted' e-mails can be retrieved and used in court
- ☐ correct spelling, punctuation and grammar
- ☐ no trivia or personal stuff
- ☐ no formatting
- ☐ reply to the right person
- ☐ don't forward e-mails from other people without permission
- ☐ don't forward e-mails with attachments

[45] See Chapter 3.

Checklist for writing business letters, memos & faxes [46]

- ☐ correct names, titles and addresses (in letters and faxes)
- ☐ detailed explanatory subject line
- ☐ subject line in bold
- ☐ no 'Re.' in subject line
- ☐ a short, simple audit-trail sentence with only one idea
- ☐ stop when you're finished
- ☐ say 'Call me...' only if you mean it
- ☐ clear in meaning
- ☐ clear in format
- ☐ concise
- ☐ concrete (specific, not vague)
- ☐ complete
- ☐ courteous
- ☐ constructive: positive
- ☐ constructive: the next action is clear
- ☐ correct facts
- ☐ correct spelling, punctuation and grammar

[46] See Chapter 3.

Checklist for writing media releases[47]

- ☐ first sentence tells the whole story (who, what, where, when)
- ☐ plug your newsworthy angle
- ☐ short words, short sentences, plain English
- ☐ strict inverted pyramid structure
- ☐ headline in present tense (as if happening now)
- ☐ headline is active
- ☐ one page maximum
- ☐ no bullet points
- ☐ include a colourful quote
- ☐ attribute all quotes
- ☐ maximum two sentences per paragraph
- ☐ mention your organisation's name early
- ☐ contact only one person per organisation
- ☐ use mail or e-mail (fax is your last resort)
- ☐ meet the deadline
- ☐ wide margins
- ☐ standard font

[47] See Chapter 3.

Checklist for writing reports: the process[48]

☐ 1. clarify the brief, purpose and scope

☐ 2. gather information

☐ 3. sort, select and analyse data

☐ 4. prepare outline using only phrases (not sentences)

☐ 5. write rough draft

☐ 6. prepare graphics

☐ 7. write executive summary

☐ 8. get feedback, revise

☐ 9. edit and proofread

[48] See Chapter 4.

Checklist for writing reports: the content[49]

- ☐ content fits purpose and scope of report
- ☐ structure: inverted pyramid
- ☐ all essential information included
- ☐ no unnecessary information
- ☐ style is easy for the intended readers
- ☐ title page gives much more than the basic facts
- ☐ table of contents is user-friendly
- ☐ descriptive, specific headings throughout
- ☐ executive summary summarises every section of report
- ☐ executive summary is interesting to read
- ☐ introduction includes brief, purpose and scope
- ☐ background in best place: in introduction, a separate section or appendix
- ☐ recommendations (if specified in the brief)
- ☐ conclusions section tells what you have deduced from the evidence
- ☐ conclusion section (if any) rounds off and summarises the discussion
- ☐ discussion section: important issues occupy the most pages
- ☐ methods section (optional)
- ☐ costs (if specified in the brief)
- ☐ appendixes (if any) labelled and named
- ☐ format follows company style guide
- ☐ if no company style guide, format is modern or a compromise

[49] See Chapter 4.

Checklist for writing proposals: the content[50]

- ☐ a covering letter
- ☐ executive summary: the entire proposal in a nutshell
- ☐ your understanding of the client's problem or need
- ☐ your client's requirements (objectives, cost)
- ☐ your brief, if any
- ☐ if a tender, all RFT requirements are fulfilled
- ☐ your solution
- ☐ how your solution benefits your client
- ☐ why this solution among other options
- ☐ comparable success stories
- ☐ references
- ☐ costs in money, time, people, other resources
- ☐ your client's return on investment
- ☐ brief company profile
- ☐ your methods, and how they fit your client's needs
- ☐ milestones and deadlines if appropriate
- ☐ your request for the contract or business

[50] See Chapter 5.

Checklist for writing procedures[51]

- ☐ say who is responsible or who does what
- ☐ cover aspects that are not in job description
- ☐ use easy-to-read format
- ☐ write steps in chronological order
- ☐ use active voice
- ☐ use short sentences
- ☐ use all other features of plain English
- ☐ explain jargon or abbreviations the first time
- ☐ provide a glossary if necessary

---

[51] See Chapter 6.

Checklist for writing policy[52]

- ☐ structure determined by needs of primary reader
- ☐ facts are accurate and complete
- ☐ brief and scope stated
- ☐ present situation clearly explained
- ☐ issues clearly and separately explained
- ☐ policy options stated
- ☐ preferred policy identified
- ☐ overt risks clearly stated
- ☐ policy takes account of political and legal repercussions
- ☐ sentences can be safely quoted out of context
- ☐ feedback accepted from the appropriate people
- ☐ you personally understand every sentence you have written
- ☐ executive summary can be understood by the general public at first reading
- ☐ plain English
- ☐ objective style
- ☐ third person only (no use of 'I', 'you', or 'we')
- ☐ concrete nouns outnumber abstract nouns[53]
- ☐ consistent verb tenses
- ☐ verbs as simple as possible
- ☐ sentences clear even if quoted out of context
- ☐ passive verbs avoided when possible
- ☐ up to 40 per cent passive verbs in sensitive discussion documents
- ☐ editing has removed inconsistencies of style
- ☐ perfect grammar, spelling, punctuation and layout

[52] See Chapter 6.

[53] In your dreams, Rachel!

Checklist for page design[54]

- ☐ plenty of white space
- ☐ a standard serif font for body text
- ☐ print that's big enough to read
- ☐ about 10-14 words per line
- ☐ line spacing of about 1.2 multiple lines
- ☐ headings in bold with space above
- ☐ no underlining except for hyperlinks
- ☐ no use of italics or very little
- ☐ no block capitals except (possibly) in headings
- ☐ text flush left and ragged right
- ☐ black print on white paper
- ☐ the page as a whole is balanced
- ☐ the page as a whole looks interesting

[54] See Chapter 7.

Checklist for writing agenda for meetings (in this order) [55]

☐ 1. apologies

☐ 2. minutes of last meeting

☐ 3. matters arising

☐ 4. financial report

☐ 5. other reports

☐ 6. correspondence (optional)

☐ 7. specific items of business

☐ 8. general business

☐ 9. time, date and place of next meeting

[55] See Chapter 8.

Checklist for writing minutes[56]

- ☐ items in the same the order as the agenda
- ☐ subheadings that correspond to agenda items
- ☐ one-sentence background to decisions
- ☐ all agreed expenses
- ☐ all agreed actions
- ☐ all agreed deadlines
- ☐ who will take each agreed action
- ☐ exact wording of formal motions
- ☐ names of proposers and seconders of formal motions
- ☐ numbers voting each way if vote is split
- ☐ names of those abstaining or voting against, if required
- ☐ facts are separated from opinions
- ☐ OPTIONAL: who said what on important issues
- ☐ indirect speech, not the exact words
- ☐ passive verbs if required

[56] See Chapter 8.

Checklist for preparing for interviews[57]

- ☐ research interviewers' organisation OR research interviewee's background
- ☐ visualise success
- ☐ rehearse answers
- ☐ prepare questions
- ☐ dress appropriately
- ☐ attend to body language

[57] See Chapter 8.

Checklist for preparing speeches and presentations[58]

- ☐ choose team leader
- ☐ allocate team roles
- ☐ write speech first as notes, using phrases, or as a mindmap
- ☐ give your key message three times
- ☐ make about three major points
- ☐ all points directly relevant to the audience's needs
- ☐ make three minor points for each major point
- ☐ start with a question, an example or the main point
- ☐ illustrate points with case histories, statistics, examples
- ☐ rehearse
- ☐ time your presentation in rehearsal
- ☐ prepare notes in phrases (on cards or electronic slides)
- ☐ check the venue, publicity, numbers
- ☐ use visual aids
- ☐ check the technology in advance
- ☐ have back-up system in case of failed technology
- ☐ visualise success
- ☐ give and receive feedback on:
  - ☐ professionalism
  - ☐ voice
  - ☐ personal manner
  - ☐ content
  - ☐ timing

[58] See Chapter 8.

Checklist for editing[59]

Stage 1

- ☐ establish document's purpose and audience
- ☐ make sure the document fulfils its purpose
- ☐ restructure the document if necessary
- ☐ make the key message obvious
- ☐ check the logic
- ☐ delete superfluous material
- ☐ write or rewrite the executive summary

Stage 2

- ☐ delete superfluous paragraphs, sentences and words
- ☐ add material that has been omitted
- ☐ rewrite headings so they are explanatory and powerful
- ☐ add extra sub-headings
- ☐ create smooth transitions between paragraphs

Stage 3

- ☐ shorten over-long sentences
- ☐ correct grammar mistakes
- ☐ reduce number of passive verbs
- ☐ replace fancy, old-fashioned or ambiguous words
- ☐ change negative language into positive language
- ☐ edit into plain English
- ☐ impose consistent style

[59] See Chapter 9.

Checklist for correct grammar and punctuation[60]

- ☐ run-on sentences
- ☐ However,
- ☐ its
- ☐ apostrophes
- ☐ 'only', 'just', 'still' and 'even'
- ☐ me, I, myself, you, yourself
- ☐ parallel lists and bullet points
- ☐ singular or plural? (each, every, the board, the committee etc)
- ☐ 'which' and 'that' clauses
- ☐ bullet point punctuation
- ☐ bullet points or numbers?
- ☐ capital letters in titles
- ☐ numbers: digits or roman letters?

[60] See Chapter 9.

Checklist for proofreading[61]

Your aim is to achieve both correctness and consistency.

	body text	headings	headers & footers	numbers	bullets & lists	graphics
fonts	☐	☐	☐	☐	☐	☐
line spacing	☐	☐	☐	☐	☐	☐
alignment	☐	☐	☐	☐	☐	☐
margins	☐	☐	☐	☐	☐	☐
spelling	☐	☐	☐	☐	☐	☐
punctu-ation	☐	☐	☐	☐	☐	☐
grammar	☐	☐	☐	☐	☐	☐
repetition	☐	☐	☐	☐	☐	☐
missing material	☐	☐	☐	☐	☐	☐
incorrect numbers	☐	☐	☐	☐	☐	☐
bad line breaks	☐	☐	☐	☐	☐	☐
bad page breaks	☐	☐	☐	☐	☐	☐

[61] See Chapter 9.

Checklist for writing quickly[62]

- ☐ think first: who is this for?
- ☐ think first: what do I want the reader to do?
- ☐ think first: what's the key message?
- ☐ omit Mr, Ms, Miss or Mrs
- ☐ mindmap or outline larger documents before you begin
- ☐ make notes in words or phrases (not sentences)
- ☐ keep your audit-trail sentence short
- ☐ use 'please' and 'thank you'
- ☐ use 'you', 'we' and 'I'
- ☐ use short sentences
- ☐ writer's block: chop the troublesome sentence in two
- ☐ writer's block: delete the troublesome sentence
- ☐ write as you speak, and then edit later
- ☐ when you can't think of the right word, leave a blank and keep writing
- ☐ use templates for reports and proposals
- ☐ use checklists

[62] See Chapter 9.

Checklist for corporate style guide: minimum content[63]

- ☐ model letter showing
  - ☐ address
  - ☐ hello phrase
  - ☐ subject line
  - ☐ goodbye phrase
  - ☐ sign-off
  - ☐ font
  - ☐ line
  - ☐ spacing
- ☐ guidelines for house style
  - ☐ use of passive
  - ☐ sentence length
  - ☐ use of 'you' and 'we' and 'I'
  - ☐ 'please' and 'thank you'
  - ☐ positive language
  - ☐ readability grade
- ☐ information about templates
- ☐ punctuation rules
- ☐ correct form of all commonly used titles, departments etc
- ☐ correct form of technical words, abbreviations and acronyms
- ☐ correct form of other words commonly used in-house

[63] See Chapter 10.

Checklist for document control[64]

- ☐ define documents that must be controlled
- ☐ document-numbering system has unique numbers
- ☐ document-numbering system identifies latest version
- ☐ set criteria for deciding who will approve each type of document
- ☐ name people authorised to approve each type of document
- ☐ ensure procedures are reviewed by all relevant parties
- ☐ set procedures for recording identities of writer/approver
- ☐ define standard style, content and pagination method for each document
- ☐ establish who needs copies of each document
- ☐ create system for removing obsolete documents
- ☐ maintain master register of all important documents
- ☐ set procedures for updating master register
- ☐ set procedures for making master register available to users
- ☐ establish a change-control system: make information available for informed decisions
- ☐ show on the document where approver should authorise the change
- ☐ set procedures for identifying changes to a document
- ☐ document all the above systems
- ☐ system covers documents coming from outside (not just generated in-house)

---

[64] See Chapter 10.

Checklist for document records control[65]

- ☐ identify records necessary to show ISO9001 conformance
- ☐ ensure data in records are identifiable with a specific product, service or event
- ☐ define period of storage for each type of record
- ☐ define person responsible for each type of record
- ☐ define where records are kept
- ☐ define whether access is restricted
- ☐ ensure suitable environment for safe storage of records
- ☐ establish a system for retrieving records
- ☐ identify disposal methods and disposal authorities
- ☐ audit system includes periodic reviews of stored records
- ☐ document computer systems processes for electronic records

[65] See Chapter 10.

More tips and articles for corporate communicators

Writing content for Web and intranet sites are a fact of life for most people who work in corporate communications.

You'll find a large archive of useful articles on this topic at the Quality Web Content site:

www.webpagecontent.com

Index